THE PERFECT LEGAL BUSINESS

Simon McCrum

BENNION
KEARNY

Published in 2025 by Bennion Kearny Limited

Woodside, Oakamoor, ST10 3AE, UK

www.BennionKearny.com

ISBN: 978-1-915855-39-8

Bennion Kearny Limited. 6 Woodside, Churnet View Road, Oakamoor, ST10 3AE, United Kingdom.

I dedicate this book to my A-Team

Angie, Murdoch, and Maverick

Books in this Series

Contents

INTRODUCTION

This book was all but completed just before the COVID pandemic brought lockdown to law firms.

It was not changed to cater for the crisis. It has not been changed since the crisis. The lessons it was evangelical about before the crisis were all the more relevant and compelling during the crisis, and they remain so now, long after the crisis.

What follows in this book is the pulling together of a thousand lessons that I have learned. I have learned them from my own trials, successes, and failures – during good times and bad. I have learned them working as a lawyer in firms not owned by me, whilst a co-owner of other firms, whilst leading many teams, and – ultimately – a large law firm. And I have learned them from the very many law firms that have brought me into their businesses over the years.

That all adds up to one hell of an education. It includes a masterclass in cutting and growing your way out of a crisis (the 2007 credit crunch) and another in wrestling with runaway growth just a few years later when my firm had become the UK's fastest-growing law firm.

I talk in this book about *The* Perfect Legal Business. A better phrase might be *A* Perfect Legal Business, as many successful firms don't look like the firm I describe here. There are highly successful firms (and teams within firms) that have no control over their pricing, and who have clients who may not be in a position to give further legal work to the firm.

Some firms may only do one work type. Hopefully, though, there is much interest, relevance, and value in this book for these firms and teams, too.

After many years engaged full-time in the management and growth of various teams at Pannone, a full-service law firm of some £50m turnover, I subsequently became Managing Partner of a £6m turnover firm, and it felt like a great opportunity to design, shape, build, and grow what I felt would be "the perfect legal business".

At the front of my mind were things like delivering a great service to clients in a particular way – every lawyer, every time, guaranteed. By this, I meant that the client would think it was a great service, not just that we, as lawyers, did. They are very different things!

Of course, I also wanted to build an environment like the one I had seen and enjoyed at Pannone, where equality and diversity reigned, and all people in the firm could thrive and progress on merit and hard work. A firm where all the team members in all their roles could rise up a career path, where lawyers and Business Support worked together closely.

I wanted to develop innovative ways of getting new clients, and I wanted to make sure that when a client came to us, they not only stayed with us but used us for everything across all our teams. It meant that existing clients were our focus, not new clients.

I wanted to create a firm that was very profitable – but my knowledge at that time told me that everything would be okay if we just kept growing.

Overall, if I had to sum it all up, I wanted to build a legal "brand" – the first true legal brand. It would be based on a promise to clients that – as a high-performing team of committed people in a large law firm – we'd look after clients in the same great way. Every lawyer, every time – guaranteed.

My belief and vision was that a full-service law firm model could then reap the huge business dividend of all clients using us for all their legal needs.

It all sounds good, doesn't it? A few things got in the way, though.

Firstly, of course, the firm had been running for many years. No existing firm has got a blank piece of paper when it comes to business growth and improvement. Change was required, and change isn't always easy.

Secondly, it was September 2007. If you look at all the graphs, that's the month the credit crunch started. It wasn't a great time to be a law firm with a big overdraft.

Thirdly, there were gaps in my knowledge and focus. I was an unashamed growth merchant, and I felt sure that profit – and I use that word deliberately, as at that time I thought in terms of "profit" rather than in terms of "cash" – would follow from the other aims. My main focus was not always on the things that most businesses "out there" are (and have to be) obsessed with – pricing, productivity, profit margins, and cash.

Fourthly, it is incredible how you can be pushed and pulled in a law firm so that you get embroiled in a thousand things other than the things you should be doing – and that's as a Managing Partner with no fee-earning responsibilities. I can't imagine what it's like if you have clients, cases, and fee targets as well.

It is easy to paper over these deficiencies in my priorities. What the hell, we became the fastest-growing law firm in the country, didn't we, out of some 10,000 firms? Correct – the law firm with the fastest-growing *turnover*. We had two years of 35% growth on the trot, for example. It felt good at the time. Our profile rose, talent flocked to our door, *profit* looked good. But I simply wouldn't do it that way again, and the Perfect Legal Business would not go about things that way.

I was (and am) very proud of many of the things we achieved, but looking back, I can see my lack of focus in other areas. I see the same lack of focus across many parts of our profession today, and I am now passionate about helping firms *see what I didn't see*. I can now see these things a mile away.

Since my firm was acquired in 2016 and I started my management consultancy business for law firms, I have become evangelical about helping law firms to do the things that we did right, and to avoid doing the things that we did wrong. I now work with firms to move them closer to becoming what I call The Perfect Legal Business, in which no one part can be fixed with overwhelming results – everything is joined together. It is easy to pull together all these "right" and "wrong" things, to lay out the skeleton of The Perfect Legal Business. I try to do that in this book.

I start from the premise that, as a firm of solicitors, we have a role and responsibility to change clients' personal and business lives for the better and that, as a business, we have a responsibility to change the lives of our people and our owners for the better, too.

The Perfect Legal Business achieves all of these things, and on top of pricing, productivity, profit, and cash, its people can have real *pride* in what it does and how it does it. All of this is within the grasp of every law firm. And quickly.

Yes, the sands are constantly shifting. Artificial Intelligence, for example, is here and *here to stay*. We need to harness this and use it – it can improve all the aspects that I talk about here. It will enhance successful, busy law firms, and hasten the demise of firms that are already struggling or arrogant in their ways. Don't let it take your eye off the ball, though; all the "usual suspect" walls are waiting to close in on law firms.

This was the first book in what became a Law Firm Management trilogy. Given the luxuries of time and experience, I came to see and understand that The Perfect Legal Business is but one leg of a tripod, where the other legs are Perfect Lawyers and Perfect Partners.

These are each covered in my books of those names, and I commend them to anyone wanting to secure a deep understanding of the forces at work, and the opportunities that are at large, in a successful law firm.

It remains remarkable to me that all the business adaptions and improvements that can lift even great law firms to higher heights are within a firm's control. The changes and improvements can start today.

In this latest edition of this first part of the trilogy, I have developed Chapter 12 to give it more force. It is "the golden ticket". I never stop thinking about how law firms can do less, better, for more, and how they can change clients' lives and change the lives of their people and their owners. Something was niggling me, and as often happens, I saw with more and more clarity that in the myriad activities that law firms spend time, energy, and money on, *this* is the acid test and *this* is the thing that they are missing.

So, if everything that is needed to secure business growth is actually under your control – not just in Chapter 12 but in all areas that I cover in this book – the trophy is literally there for the taking. It's madness not to grab it. So, grab it!

Simon McCrum, 2025

CHAPTER 1

SOME BASICS

Let's start at the shallow end of the PLB "pool" and wade out towards deeper waters.

The Perfect Legal Business does not come about by accident or by evolution, but by steady revolution. Often, big changes are needed. Revolution needs inspiring leadership to start the ball rolling and it needs the people to be right behind it for it to be sustainable.

We are indeed talking about revolution here. We are talking about throwing established practises and priorities out the window. Some firms have thrown some of them out of the window already, but the revolution is only complete when the full set has been defenestrated.

Who is going to lead it? You might be afraid at this early stage that I'm going to be looking at new-fangled algorithm-driven robots that replace human lawyers, which would need some bright young revolutionary dynamo to force through frightening new forces that no one like me would understand.

On the contrary, you will quickly come to see in this book that I am advocating a focus on the very things that most solicitors hold dear. Things like putting the client first, changing their lives for the better, delivering an excellent service, making sure that hard work is rewarded within a firm, charging clients a decent price, making a good profit, and putting something back into society. There is nothing in this book to be afraid of.

The person or people required to lead a firm as it moves towards becoming The Perfect Legal Business, therefore, are far more simply defined.

They have to be proud, hard-working, fair, focused, and utterly accepting of the fact that they are the servant of a higher authority – the business.

I cannot for certain tell a firm how it can become The Perfect Legal Business, though I have a good go at that in this book. I can, though, tell a firm how it can make sure it *never* becomes the Perfect Legal Business. That's much easier!

The first way a firm can avoid becoming the Perfect Legal Business is to make sure that decision-making is slow and turgid. The traditional partnership structure is just the job for this – make sure everyone is involved in every decision. Paralysis at Management level will guarantee failure.

When I joined my last firm as an Equity Partner, but also as Managing Partner coming in from outside, this was the result of an incredible decision by the existing owners that not only would they bring in a Managing Partner from outside but also – that if they were to truly change – the incoming Managing Partner had to have real authority. The newcomer couldn't achieve anything if they had their hands tied by partnership discussions and committee decisions. The phrase that one of my soon-to-be co-owners used when pushing this was that the new Managing Partner was there to have power, not to count paperclips.

So, a firm needs fleetness of foot and agility when it comes to making decisions. That involves the owners charging one or more of their number (but hopefully not many more than one) – or even someone who is *not* one of their number – with leading the charge and empowering that person or those persons to make decisions. The safety valve here is, of course, that if that person or persons make more wrong decisions than right decisions over a reasonable period, or they lose the dressing room, they can be relieved of the role. But they have to be given a chance.

And don't expect them to achieve great things if they are also expected to have a full caseload. Or half a caseload. In my view, and based on my experience, a good leader with suitable empowerment can make more sustainable profit for a law firm than they could ever personally bill.

Even this early "stuff" takes a firm into choppy waters, though, where there is a lack of unity of direction and lack of unity of interest at the owner level. If you have a Partner approaching retirement, they'll understandably have differing priorities to a Partner in his or her 30s or 40s who wants to invest for growth over the next few decades.

To start, let alone complete the revolution, there needs to be leadership – by an owner, by a non-owner CEO, or by a Board – that can unite all owners behind a cause that may suit some more than others.

I have read that in terms of leadership, we are in the "post-heroic" phase – business leaders no longer have to be the one person in an organisation who does everything and who deserves or takes all the glory. "Post-heroic" leadership conjures up images of a consultative, collaborative, listening kind of leader. I can see how that would produce greater team effort and personal development within a team. Law firms are different to other businesses, though. The ownership of a law firm by a number of Partners – sometimes a high number of Partners – adds to the complexity.

In reply to the question, "What kind of management structure is best for a law firm?" I always look to a musical analogy.

Take a jazz band – relaxed, casual, with everyone doing things their way. It's hard to see who the leader of the band is – there might not even be one.

That may work for a jazz band, but I am convinced it's no way to move a firm of solicitors towards being The Perfect Legal Business. Quite apart from the fact that there needs to be a focus on a fixed number of initiatives that are all done in a certain way, rather than in the free-style approach of a jazz band, lawyers, Partners, and team leaders are all prone in our profession to have very strong views on how they are going to do things – often being determined to do things "their way". Give them an inch…

Now, compare the jazz band to an orchestra. Sat within the ranks of the musicians in an orchestra may be world-class pianists or violinists, but they all look to the conductor to ensure essentially the direction of travel and the speed of travel of the piece they are playing. In their role, the conductor does nothing to diminish the standing or repute of the violinist – quite the opposite.

The violinist recognises that without that overall guidance (and leadership) from the conductor, they'd be part of a shambles rather than part of an exquisite team. This is a far more relevant and effective model for law firms that wish to perform to a high level and to change up a gear.

Next, there needs to be universal acceptance by everyone at the law firm that we operate in a highly regulated environment. It is our licence to practise. It is our quality mark over the various pretenders "out there". It is our licence to make money and – if you are The Perfect Legal Business – to print money. These regulations are our friend, not our enemy. Lawyers make a good living out of interpreting rules and small print but baulk when any apply to them.

Why, in many firms, is compliance with the firm's policies and with professional policies seen as optional? And Partners and team leaders can be the worst offenders. So much Management time and so much of the Business Support team's time is spent making up for the fact that lawyers haven't complied with internal and external rules and regulations. Who do these people think they are?

The next "basic" feature of The Perfect Legal Business would have many an investor or entrepreneur running for the hills. If you said to them, "Look, you really should buy into a law firm at a cost of hundreds of thousands of pounds, *though we can't be sure that the business will even be here next year*". What would they do? Correct.

But this is how it is with law firms. On paper, they are literally year-to-year businesses. And the reason that they are so, is Professional Indemnity Insurance. It lasts 12 months at a time – 18 months at the most. And when it comes to renewal… no insurance, no lights on. And whilst it's easy to think your firm could never rack up a dangerous claims record on the types of work that you do, I can tell you that if you haven't had the pleasure of dealing with the PII impact of a poor lawyer doing everyday work, you haven't lived.

So, having risk management as an obsession is another part of The Perfect Legal Business. Be fussy about what cases and what clients you take on. The bigger the fee, the more wary you should be. Be fussy about what lawyers you take on and what lawyers you keep on. Be obsessed with quality control and supervision and training – don't just pay lip service to these things, and don't be satisfied with a tick-box exercise just before the Lexcel inspector arrives.

All of this gets us to the starting line of our journey, the destination of which is the Perfect Legal Business. We now move on to look at the key to making the revolution sustainable – people.

CHAPTER 2

POWER TO THE PEOPLE

The people in a law firm are the beginning, the middle, and the end of everything. Or rather, their behaviours and attitudes are. The Perfect Legal Business totally embraces all values around equality and diversity, and it harnesses, develops, and promotes hard work and positive attitudes. Nothing less will do.

This takes some doing, though. Not all people's behaviours are great, and not all people's attitudes are positive. I have even heard it said that some behaviours and attitudes can be more prevalent amongst lawyers than in other walks of life – surely not?

If you bring a random set of people together into a law firm, with no common vision or direction, no clear values and "rules", and no common understanding of *why* everyone is there, and everyone is allowed to behave how they want (and they have been so allowed for decades), you end up with a certain kind of creature.

If you then omit a strong management overlay, which guides behaviours, which guides the firm's direction of travel, which makes sure that the business has people (and only has people) who will give it what a thriving business needs, you end up with a firm where there is no conformity and nothing tangible that anyone can actually buy into. People will typically buy into themselves.

The result is siloed behaviours that are anything but team-like, destructive behaviours and a tolerance of destructive behaviours, empires, and people generally doing things their way with all the missed opportunities and collateral damage that goes with that.

Growth of the business only makes things worse, as the firm brings more and more people of varied make-up and behaviours into the firm without truly inducting them into a particular way of doing things.

Compare a firm like that to one made up of only positive people, free of well-poisoners, full of people who work hard and who support their team-mates to the hilt, all of whom are working to a plan.

If the two firms were rowing boats of the racing variety, one would be going around in circles with the crew competing with and plotting against each other, and the other would be powering through the water with the whole crew smiling. In The Perfect Legal Business, not only is everyone rowing, but everyone is rowing hard, and everyone is rowing hard in the same direction. It is unstoppable.

To get to that happy state, though, a law firm has to have a vision and a set of values that support that vision. These are needed to set a new-start firm on the right road, and they are needed all the more if transformation or strengthening of an existing firm is required. It needs to be able to articulate not just what it does (which is what most law firm websites major on) but also *how* it does it, *why* it does it, and *what* it needs from its people to enable it to do it.

The people in the firm need to be and act like one team – not lots of individuals or lots of teams – and there has to be zero tolerance of contrary behaviours. Many is the time when I have worked with teams and firms where we had to start at one end of this journey and move towards a better place. It needs an iron will and no little courage. I have often described the process as walking up a see-saw. It's hard work, but there is always a moment when you know you are heading in a good direction – when the see-saw tips the other way.

It is a truly uplifting exercise where you take a sometimes conflict-ridden and sometimes poor-performing group of people, and they transform into a much happier, better-performing team.

This is done by changing the people, or – if they won't change – by changing the people.

In a business where issues like these are not addressed, the result is not just like a car driving with the handbrake on, but the car will also have a poorly-running engine as well, with no Sat Nav, where everyone is arguing over who gets to sit in the front. It'll have plenty of passengers but not enough drivers.

Having resolved that its people will all be of high quality and positive and team-like in their approach, The Perfect Legal Business makes sure that it only recruits people of this type and that it also retains all these great people. It will also make them better and better – for themselves and for the business. It invests time and money in their development. It offers the rewards (including security) that a successful business can offer.

And it offers them a visible and transparent career path. Great people need somewhere to go – or they will go. And not just a career path that is "off-the-shelf", but one where the priorities of the business are enshrined, pushed, monitored, and rewarded. All those positive people embracing and driving the business's clear priorities will mean that those priorities are inevitably achieved. In the case of The Perfect Legal Business, those priorities will become clear as you work your way through this book.

All of this adds up to something really quite spectacular – something that has an external impact in addition to its huge internal effect. Namely, an enviable Employer Brand. Not only does a strong and positive Employer Brand help a firm retain talent and, by definition, develop that talent to new heights, but it also acts as a beacon out there in the competitive talent marketplace. Great people want more than money – they want challenges, security, opportunities, investment, and to be part of a great team. They want to work with other great people. They also want a direction that they can believe in and be part of pushing and building.

As I've worked with teams over the years in order to get them into great shape, Management has often been wary of addressing performance or behavioural issues because they feared this might destabilise the good people in the team. Not a chance! The good people know they are good and they know who is swinging the lead. Good people positively light up when they see that they are at last in a team where performance will be recognised and rewarded. They resolve to stay, not to go.

I talk a lot below about how The Perfect Legal Business has strong differentiators that add up to a brand when it comes to competing for clients, but these are no more important than the need for differentiators that add up to a brand when it comes to competing to retain and attract talent. Try building a strong legal business without great people. And then try growing it without further great people.

Pausing there, we've started. We've looked at some of the basic foundations that are needed before we can focus on a number of particular building blocks that make The Perfect Legal Business stand out from the crowd.

CHAPTER 3

THE NEED FOR GROWTH

A principle that differentiates between law firms that are Perfect Legal Business material and those that are not, is their shyness around or their disinterest in "growth", and the existence or absence of "growth".

"Growth" to me is an over-arching oxygen that moves a law firm in the right direction in a sustainable way. "Growth" has a very particular and central place in the legal industry. In the client and recruitment markets, you could be forgiven for feeling like you didn't count for anything as a law firm if you aren't "growing".

I believe that any business has to "grow" to stay strong. "Growth", though, is absolutely vital in a law firm, as I hope to demonstrate here. But growth in what?

Growth in a law firm's general activity levels, growth in client numbers, growth in the "noise" that a firm can create, growth in profile, growth in turnover, growth in the number of offices, growth in the number of Partners, growth in the number of work-types offered, growth in the number of lawyers named in the directories as "leaders", growth in awards won, and growth in staff numbers can all have a positive effect. These are the things that are almost universally recognised in our industry as the badges of a successful, growing law firm. They are all the stuff of press releases, awards submissions, and staff conferences. They attract talent. They create profile and "noise".

I had growth in all of these areas – and a lot of it. But there are some key "growth" dimensions that are glaring omissions from the above list.

More than that, if the above are the only growth indicators that you pursue or measure or realise, then far from succeeding, these apparent "successes" can actually move your business towards choppy waters.

The reason is that the areas of growth listed above can all too easily go hand in hand with other, less palatable forms of "growth" – growth in debtors, growth in your overdraft, growth in borrowings more widely, growth in Equity Partner dissatisfaction that rising "profits" don't lead to rising drawings, and growth in the pressure on Senior Management and on the Business Support functions who are running faster and faster to try to keep up with the constant inflow of new people and change.

But whilst it might be easy to start a new business from scratch, and to set a course towards rapid growth in a way that these dangers and risks are avoided, the reality of seeking increased but safe growth is very different in a large vessel that is a long-established legal business with complex personnel and personal relationships and a history of doing things in a certain way.

A law firm is fraught with challenges to growth, and there are countless obstacles in the way of the change that is needed to bring and accelerate the right sort of growth. Consider the following list of challenges – which could be much longer.

Challenges to growth in a law firm

- Owners are often of different ages and, therefore, have different agendas and priorities

- Managing Partners often have caseloads so they can justify their existence

- The partnership model doesn't always bring "fleetness of foot" and can lead to paralysis

- Often, a firm has no choice but to compete on price

- There is often no quality control over the legal work that is carried out

- Lawyers in some teams sometimes don't trust lawyers in other teams

- Billing is the prime KPI – low pricing, low chargeable hours, and write-offs are overlooked

- Lawyers often talk about "my client" instead of "our client"

- Some work is "in production" for an awfully long time before it generates cash

- Some work requires law firms to fund high levels of disbursements

- Everyone can deliver their service (or not deliver their service) as they wish

- Lawyers can price the work as they wish

- Lawyers can bill the work as they wish – and can discount WIP

- Morale may be poor, and there might be a high staff turnover across the firm

- Partner behaviours might make things worse if they don't lead by example

- There is often a push for every team to market itself

- Every new client win is celebrated – regardless of whether that client will be profitable

- It often doesn't matter if Team Leaders don't grow their business

- Compliance with policies is effectively optional – and Partners can be the worst

- A firm can have too many cases – files sit in storage for weeks on a lawyer's desk

- A firm can have too many clients – it can't begin to understand and develop them

- Troublesome members of staff or poor lawyers (or Partners) are often tolerated

- Lawyers are rewarded on billings alone

- Only "bills out" counts – debtors are for Credit Control to sort out

- Clients are seen just as cases, owned by the lawyer dealing with the case

- The client journey is often short-lived because service is no better than "average" and bills are high

- Clients are never asked how the firm is doing during the case

- Cash is always tight so there is no investment

- Pay might be behind that of competitor firms

- There might be no clear career path

- There is little focus on developing existing clients

- The way forward is often seen as "more marketing!" – winning more new clients (on price)

- The Marketing team have no ammunition to set the firm apart from competitors

- The firm tries to *sell* things to clients – not extend care proactively to them

- No one really knows where the firm is making or losing money

The list could go on. It's hard work growing a law firm, isn't it? How on earth do you achieve the desired and vital growth in the face of even a small number of these challenges?

The short answer is that you simply have to overcome any challenges you face, for real dangers await the law firm that doesn't achieve growth – growth that is, of course, the right sort.

CHAPTER 4

IS "PROFIT" GROWTH
THE RIGHT GROWTH?

So, what is the right sort of growth? All the growth types mentioned in the previous chapter can be growth of the right sort, PROVIDED ALWAYS (forgive the lawyer speak) that those forms of growth are accompanied by growth in some key additional areas. That is, in hard business areas.

Ah, you mean we need growth in "profit"? (I apologise if I am teaching you to suck eggs. I have, however, seen more than enough people in law firms at even middle- and senior-management levels who do not grasp the following basics. It took a baptism of fire and a lot of sleepless nights for me to truly learn about these things.)

Not everyone understands that "profit" and "cash" are very different things – particularly in law firms. If they have heard that these are different things, they might not fully understand *why* that is so. A good friend of mine in the legal sector once explained all of this to a law firm Managing Partner, whose reply was, "Bloody hell – when did they change that?"

In a law firm, you make a profit in two ways – and you don't have any choice about that. It's the law.

Both of them can fool you completely.

First, in the simplest of terms, if you bill say £100 (plus, in some parts of the world, VAT, or some other sales tax) in a year and you pay staff and suppliers say £60, then you have made a profit of £40.

But what if those £100 of bills haven't been paid? You have still made a profit, but you will run out of cash. You will die a profitable business. Many businesses that die are profitable.

Worse than that, depending on where you are in the world, for VAT-registered law firms, when you raised that £100 of bills, depending on your size and on timings, you might have to use a further £20 of your *own* cash to pay the VAT. Even before your clients have paid you, you are paying out further money over and above the lawyers' salaries and all your overheads. That £20 may not sound like a lot, but in a firm with unpaid bills of say £250,000 – and there are a lot of them – that is VAT of £50,000 that has to be found, depending on location and timings.

Worse still, as these bills form part of your profit, you have to pay tax on that profit. Out of your own money, if you leave these bills unpaid.

It's insanity, isn't it? And yet our profession is pressured, as my firm was, with debtor books that mean that your hard work is funding your clients' businesses, while you grind away watching your cash deplete just as you are doing "well". Success can kill you.

A sure-fire way of killing a law firm is to issue lots of bills and then allow extended credit terms to your clients. Yes, this first type of profit will be going up, and you'll be doing well on paper. But cash will be pouring out in terms of salaries, VAT perhaps, and overheads, and then in the shape of tax on your "profit". Your very growth in profit will do you in, in the end. It's actually got a name – the business world calls it "over-trading" – but I prefer to call it being blinded by hollow success.

The first thing I now do when I start an engagement with a law firm is to ask to see their Debtors ledger. If their "way" is to focus on billings alone, and they live with an Aged Debtors book which has columns headed 0-30 days, 30-60 days, 60-90 days, 90-120 days, and yes, 120+ days, I immediately re-calibrate my focus. Any growth in their lawyer numbers, Partner numbers, teams, offices, and clients will do them harm, not good.

But it gets worse. The second way that a law firm makes "profit" is even more dangerous. In most firms, there will be a lot of work and time recorded "on the system". Under our laws, a law firm has to value that Work in Progress, or WIP, on the first day of every financial year to arrive at an Opening Value. Then, it has to value it again on the last day of every financial year to arrive at a Closing Value. If the Closing Value is higher than the Opening Value, the difference (or the WIP Uplift) has to be added to your profit, pound for pound.

Sounds good? "Hey, we haven't even billed that work and our profit's gone up!"

Actually, it's not good at all. Profit (of both types) gets taxed, of course. You thus have to pay tax (that is, pay it in cash) on this profit, too – but you haven't billed the client yet, let alone been paid. So, guess whose money is going to be used to pay the tax? Yours. Yet another drain on your limited bucket of cash.

As you can see, there are two types of profit, but neither is the only stuff that counts – cash.

And here's an interesting thing that has caught many a law firm out. It became a common expectation amongst law firms that the WIP Closing Value would always be higher at the end of a firm's financial year than the WIP Opening Value had been at its start, so that there would always be a WIP *uplift*. But what happens if the WIP Closing Value is *lower* than the WIP Opening Value at the end of a financial year? The answer is that the reduction is applied, pound-for-pound, to the first type of profit that we looked at above, *reducing* the firm's profit.

This can turn a profit-making firm (and possibly even a cash-rich, profit-making firm) into a loss-maker.

It can be a nightmare, and I came to call it the "WIP Monster" as it always seems to be lurking and ready to lay us low.

You can maybe see more clearly now why keeping WIP at a minimum (by billing it regularly – and getting those bills paid) and why writing off dead WIP and accurately valuing any WIP at year-end that can't be billed at that point are both vital to arriving at an accurate picture of a law firm's finances.

The profit that a firm actually wants is billing-based profit, not WIP-based profit, but where those bills are paid quickly.

There's a very useful "speedometer" that you can use that tells you exactly how efficient a team is at making this right kind of profit, and whether their efforts to increase that profit are working – it's called the Team Gross Margin. I'll come to this later, but first, let me dwell a little longer on a point I have just made. The bills really do need to be paid quickly. Let's talk more about *cash*.

CHAPTER 5

CASH

In the same way, and to exactly the same degree that a human needs oxygen, a business needs cash. Cash, not just profit. They are different things. Profit is no substitute for oxygen.

And a law firm needs an awful lot of cash. Every month.

Running a law firm can easily become no more than an exercise in counting "cash in" and "cash out" – on a daily let alone a monthly basis. The monthly salary bill in a law firm, for example, is completely out of kilter when set against other non-law businesses with a similar headcount. Law firms have a voracious appetite for cash, each and every month. It never stops. And if you try to grow by bringing in new lawyers or teams or offices, from Month #1 of any such enterprise, your cash appetite goes through the roof (whilst it may take you until say Month #6 before those lawyers start bringing in any cash).

A firm can roughly work out what its monthly break-even cash figure is – how much cash is going to go out – which should dictate how much incoming cash is needed. Not all firms seem to work it out, though. Do you know your cash break-even figure? It is amazing how many firms can't tell me in even rough terms what their break-even cash figure each month is. Do you know how many months your available oxygen would last if no more cash came in? Such is the ocean of cash that flows out of law firms that, for many law firms, a couple of difficult trading months would bring real anguish.

The problem with cash, of course, is that a business only has a limited amount of the stuff. Most law firms are small or medium-sized enterprises. They are typically owner-managed businesses.

The cash that most law firms have access to is usually limited to the sum of the cash that the owners have put into or left in the business on the one hand, and money that the bank lets it use by way of an overdraft on the other.

Whilst a reduction in profit and cash are certainly ways to take a law firm in the wrong direction, so it follows that an increase in profit and an increase in cash are vital to take a law firm in the right direction.

All the forms of growth that I mentioned in Chapter 3 are fine, but they are in fact dangerous if they are not accompanied on the growth bus by an increase in cash reserves (which flows from a growth in profit of the right type – see above).

This is all the more important when we remind ourselves that The Perfect Legal Business is made up of great people – great Partners, great lawyers, and a Business Support team at the top of its game. There's a lot more to it than money, but great people usually command great salaries – and expect growing salaries – as a reward for ongoing loyalty and hard work. Great people don't take "standing still" in reward terms too well, particularly when their marketplaces are buoyant, and there always seem to be competitor law firms out there with fat chequebooks.

Whilst this may sound hard-nosed, and you may be thinking, "So, it's all about the money, is it?", yes it absolutely is. But let's embrace that rather than run away from it. I've been in law firms that had a lot of money and in firms that have not had a lot of money. I know where I'd rather be, and I know where the people were happier.

I am – now – *all* about the money, but as you will see in this book, I am also passionate about there being another side to the coin, if you excuse the pun.

So, a first step down the road towards The Perfect Legal Business is to recognise that it is all about GROWTH IN CASH. No cash means no choices, no freedom – and frankly, no sleep.

If a law firm does not achieve growth each year in profit and, more importantly, in cash terms, then one inevitable impact, because there is always only a limited supply of cash, is that it has to control its costs going forward. And those costs don't even stay the same every year. There seems to be universal upward pressure on salaries and on suppliers' prices – whether that be paper, professional indemnity insurance, rent, IT costs, etc, even where we aren't even talking about major investments or upgrades.

So, to even *stand still*, a law firm has to *grow* in profit and cash terms. If you then accept that your great people are vulnerable if they don't believe they are in the right place to enjoy increasing rewards (i.e., pay raises and wider investment in them and their development) year after year, then you can see – to an even greater degree – that there has to be profit and cash growth if the firm is to remain on a healthy, forward-only trajectory.

Standing still is a suicide note for a law firm – and not a very long suicide note at that.

If you, as a law firm leader or manager, are scratching your head wondering why things feel tight just as billing and profit are looking great, look no further than this book, and you are not alone. I have been there, and I have seen and still see many law firms there.

The fact that your profit looks good means nothing. It could be based on unpaid bills and/or on WIP Uplift, rather than on cash. "Profit" can be dangerously misleading. Your billing could be high, but so could your WIP and so could your debtors.

These things can make you relax because "profit" looks good, rather than making you drive growth in profit, based on paid bills.

That is quite apart from the fact that if a chunk of your year-end profit is based on WIP Uplift, you've still got to find the cash to pay the tax on that part of your profit.

It is easy to be comforted by a team's headline billing or even profit figures that, on the face of it, give reasons to be cheerful.

Take a high-billing, high-performing, growing, "profitable" team. That team could, in fact, be hurting you.

Hard to believe? It's not enough to look at their profitability. You also need to look at their *cash impact.*

We used something that I called a Cash Impact Statement, which looked at the overall impact of a team on the *cash* (i.e., on the oxygen) of the business. We need to lift the bonnet and look beyond the "big billing" or "big profit" headlines. This tool was a very helpful but very sobering instrument. A team's Cash Impact Statement looked like this:

Team	Year-to-Date Cash Position (£)
Billings	
Less unpaid bills	
Less VAT paid on their unpaid bills (if relevant)	
Less disbursements paid out and not yet recovered	
Less disbursements written off	
Less salaries, PAYE, NI, Pensions, Etc	
Less team marketing spend	
Less practising certificates, training, etc	
Team's net cash impact	

Using this tool, I could look at a team and see the degree to which they were *truly* helping or hindering our business at any point in our financial year, *regardless* of how they were doing in billing or profit terms.

A team may be profitable but may, at the same time, be really holding your business back by draining it of cash.

I was able to show at the end of Month #9, for example, that one huge team of lawyers had, overall, brought in less cash to the firm than a one-lawyer team in another area of work.

This all underlines the area that your business needs to focus on – it's *always* cash generation and cash collection.

Start running without breathing, without oxygen, and see how far you get.

Where a team is in a "steady" phase, without any significant recruitment going on, the Cash Impact challenge is a real one.

But step out of the "steady" phase into any kind of "growth" phase and watch what happens. As soon as you add new recruits to a team, the cash outflow increases, and the cash impact of the team starts worsening on the day the new lawyer or lawyers arrive (with all the follow-on costs that go with recruitment). And yes – hopefully the new lawyers will do some bills quite soon – but absent fast payment of those bills, they add to the problem.

These are all aspects to be borne in mind when growth is pursued by recruiting lawyers from other firms – as a route to growth, it is not always a road paved with gold and is often a road paved with pain.

We thus arrive at one of the first features of the Perfect Legal Business – it has at its core, like any non-law business, a hunger not just for profit but for *cash* growth. The hunger is a focused hunger. Without growth each year in profit *and cash*, a cash-hungry business like a law firm begins to become short of breath – panting and wheezing and slowing down, instead of carrying on the forward charge.

Finally, here, while I say the Perfect Legal Business puts cash "front of house", and it sets out at the start of every financial year to achieve increased profit and cash reserves by the end of the year, there are the aforementioned two sides to this coin.

I believe that it's perfectly in order and absolutely nothing to be ashamed of to charge a high price for your legal services, and to bill for every minute your lawyers spend on a file, and to insist on quick payment of bills – that is, to take a hard approach that puts your business first – provided you are discharging the role that I believe law firms and solicitors have in society. That is, to make the personal and business lives of clients better.

So, yes, I'm now a disciple of putting money front of house and of growing profit and more importantly cash, but I'm a disciple of doing this by giving your people and your clients something invaluable in return.

The first step on our journey is now clear – The Perfect Legal Business secures growth in profit *and cash* each financial year. To not accept that, and to not have these as your top priorities, risks everything that you are doing in place of these things.

How on earth do you secure such growth, though?

CHAPTER 6

HOW FIRMS TRY TO ACHIEVE THIS "RIGHT" GROWTH

Accepting that growth in profit and cash is key, I have seen law firms try to "grow" their businesses in the following ways:

- Bringing in a new Partner (with a "following")

- Bringing in a team of lawyers from another firm

- Encouraging (or demanding) people to do more "BD"

- Opening a new practise area

- Opening a new office

- Increasing prices

- Merging with a local competitor

- Acquiring small local firms

- Pushing each team to have its own marketing plan

- Building a new website

- Designing new brochures

- Advertising or sponsorship campaigns

- Spending more on their marketing team

- Social media campaigns

- Press releases

Before we look at how the Perfect Legal Business really can grow its profit and cash, let's look at the effectiveness of, and the impact of, some of these common "growth" strategies, particularly if they are not carefully managed. Even if they succeed, they don't necessarily bring the growth in profit and cash terms that the Perfect Legal Business needs. Instead, they can bring an uplift in danger.

Bringing in new lawyers from other firms

Generally, the statistics around the success of lateral hires (bringing in Partners or teams from other firms) do not make good reading. History is littered with stories of the behaviours of Partners from one firm that didn't quite fit in with the behaviours at the new firm, as well as stories of "star" hires that didn't quite live up to expectations.

I have, though, seen some great examples of firms using a determined, focused recruitment programme as a main growth strategy. Some firms have this as the backbone of their growth aspirations. There are some clear features present in such firms, though, which lead to these programmes being effective and successful while other firms fail at it.

A commitment to a culture, and a set of values and behaviours is key. If someone doesn't fit, then their clients and fees are not welcome. Longer-term, these firms can see that not all that glitters is gold.

That is carried through the recruitment programme by the consistency of assessment and even interviewer involvement at the interview stages – lawyers of random make-up are not being recruited in different parts of the firm by interview panels of random make-up.

Once hired, new recruits are well and truly inducted into the new firm. Induction is about more than fire exits.

And wrong moves on the part of the new arrivals are acted upon so that education and induction are an ongoing process, not a series of meetings that are signed off by the Head of HR or the office manager after a week.

Firms that make the recruitment strategy work also have the ability to recognise where a new hire simply isn't working and won't ever work, and such firms are ready, willing, and able to make a hard business decision to draw a line and terminate a new or recent hire.

And, finally, such firms recognise the cash implications of achieving growth in this way. A further benefit of their strong cash behaviours is that a sustained recruitment programme is possible.

If a firm doesn't have a set of values and behaviours that make up a clear culture, and/or does not recognise the potential cash impact of new hires, then "recruitment" as a growth strategy is very dangerous. It can lead to a real cash challenge and to long-term cultural erosion – particularly if it is difficult for Management to be seen to have failed in a senior hire. The outpouring of cash continues, and behaviours are left unaddressed, to avoid the firm having to go "back to square one" or to avoid Management having egg on its face.

Let's look at the cash dangers that a "growth-by-recruitment" strategy can bring if the hiring firm doesn't already embrace the right cash behaviours, and doesn't imbue these into every incoming lawyer from the outset.

It may be that – at their former firms – the lawyers, Partners or team in question were rewarded, as is largely the way in our profession, for their billing levels. It would be surprising if they were not. That's all you asked them about in the interview, right? (You mean you didn't ask them about debtor days, team Gross Margin, and WIP write-offs?)

So, they start at your firm and, of course, their (high) salaries – which are paid in *cash* – start going out in the first month. If things go well, they start billing after a month or two or three, depending on the type of work they do. In some work-types, the delay before billing starts can be much, much longer.

But how quickly are their clients used to paying those bills when they start getting sent out? What were the cash behaviours and disciplines of the lawyer's previous firm? Do their clients (who may well be having cashflow challenges of their own) see this as an opportunity to have suppliers (you) fund their business for longer?

A few months of big salaries going out without more cash than that coming in, and that new lateral hire or that new team can start causing you cash problems – even though their billing and, thus, your "profit" may look healthy. The position is all the more damaging if the lawyers in question do what I call "long-tail" work – long commercial or property deals, or litigation that is of a contingent nature, for example. It doesn't take many of these large salaries before limited cash reserves get depleted in the face of locked-up WIP and/or unpaid bills – and it's even worse if all the while you are paying VAT on their unpaid bills and tax on any WIP-based profit. At today's salary levels, recruitment hurts if cash doesn't start flowing in from the new lawyer or lawyers quickly.

As I say, though, some firms use the recruitment process really well as a vehicle for significant growth, but it is not always gold-plated and is not guaranteed to be successful.

Many firms will have been bowled over by the promised "followings" or Business Development brilliance of lawyers and Partners they have interviewed, only for reality to subsequently fall a long way short of the rainbows that were promised.

Even where a new hire does deliver, a new Partner or team that is under pressure to perform (in the first instance, to open files) will not necessarily be committed to charging "top dollar" for their work. They'll just be relieved to get another job in. Without clear expectations and established behaviours on the part of the hiring firm, the new lawyers are unlikely to get their clients to follow them with an assurance that hourly rates will be increasing.

On the contrary, the new lawyers may be hoping to coax their clients across to the new firm by telling them prices will be going down.

Moreover, those clients are unlikely to welcome a decrease in the credit terms that will be extended to them. The wheels of their transition to the new firm will be oiled by the promise of lower prices and longer credit terms. I have seen very many examples of new Partners whose performance was celebrated – until Management looked at their "Debtors" printout. Bear in mind, too, (from what I said above) that any VAT has to be paid even if the client hasn't paid the bill. A new high-billing team that doesn't get their bills paid quickly will really start hurting you.

Securing growth by new and increased "Marketing" and by "Business Development"

I've always liked the saying, "Only half of all BD and Marketing works – but you never know which half".

I believe that when it comes to law firms, more than half of all BD and Marketing does *not* work. I believe a great deal *more* than half doesn't work and is a waste of time, money, energy, and the goodwill that a firm's people invest in it.

If we step outside the legal sector for a moment, I'll show you what I mean.

Imagine two companies that both make cars, where there is nothing different between the cars of Company

A and the cars of Company B. They are priced roughly the same, too. As it happens, the cars of both Company A and Company B break down from time to time. Sometimes, you get a good one; sometimes, you get a bad one.

Let's imagine how the meeting between the Senior Management Team at Company A, and their Marketing and their Sales teams go.

It would not be unusual for the CEO to demand more and more Marketing and more and more Sales effort to get sales up. The more marketing, the better, right?

Now, imagine you're the Marketing or Sales team. You'd be faced with a huge challenge: "What on earth can we say about our cars that'll get people to buy them?" They're in a fix, as they can't differentiate their cars in any way from those of Company B. How amazing it would be if they could boast about the quality and reliability of their cars – what a differentiator that would be. But theirs break down, too.

So, what's left in terms of ammunition that they can use? Not much, really. Maybe "Our cars are cheaper"?

Or maybe they could try what lots of law firms try – they could tell customers how long they've been in business. Or they could showcase the industry awards they've won. Or they could boast about being a really big car maker – in the Top 200 carmakers in the country. But absent real differentiators between their cars and those of their competitors – differentiators that really benefit customers – you can see that the Marketing people have an uphill struggle.

That's precisely how it is for the Marketing people in law firms.

In very general terms, I think we can divide "Marketing" (in the sense that it is used in law firms) into Part 1 and Part 2.

- Part 1 is the design and the engineering of real differentiators – outstanding aspects that set a firm apart in a crowded marketplace which are of real value to clients.

- Part 2 is the broadcasting of the firm's messages to existing clients and to potential clients.

I have rarely seen *any* Part 1 work *at all* for a law firm. Instead, law firms spend a fortune on Part 2 activities without building any real brand, promise, or differentiators. In reality, a fortune is expended shouting about, well, not much at all.

In the business world more widely, Marketing often leads the way. They have input into the *"what"* and also into the *"how"* and into the *"why"* of a business. They help to shape the culture, the values, the design, and the pricing of goods and services. They thus engineer a brand and they help to build differentiators that give a boost to the business's marketing and Business Development efforts.

In the example given above, it would not be unusual for the Marketing people at Company A to engage with the CEO to underline that the real brand opportunity here was to build a car that *didn't* break down. Imagine the messaging that could then be broadcast. "Our cars will get you there!" And guess what could happen to the price of their cars and the number that they sold.

In law firms, typically because of the respective seniority of Partners and Marketing people that still exists in most practises, the Marketing people are led by the lawyers and do what the lawyers ask them – let's have a seminar, let's have a cheese & wine evening, or let's write an article, etc. And then nothing arrives from the lawyers until the last minute. And no one's ever sure who to invite to events once they've been organised. It's all pretty ad hoc, but it doesn't cause any real problems because that's exactly what's going on at a lot of competitor firms.

The Marketing team usually just doesn't have the standing to say, for example, "Why don't we completely re-design the service that we offer clients, so that we innovate to deliver a truly great service – every lawyer, every time. That'll make us a brand with a promise that will have people flocking to us and that will be *the* differentiator in the legal market. We can charge a fortune for it".

Absent that kind of standing on the part of the Marketing team in a law firm, what *can* the Marketing people possibly say that sets *their* lawyers apart from those of other law firms? And what *can* the lawyers themselves who are charged with doing "Business Development" and "Networking" say that is going to first capture someone's interest at a networking event and then enable that contact to be nurtured so that they become a life-long client (apart from "We're really good" or "We're really cheap")?

When we look at law firm differentiators in the next chapter, you can see exactly what law firms currently say to "stand out" in a crowded market.

Pursuing growth by driving each team to undertake marketing and BD efforts

It is not uncommon for each team in a law firm to be allocated its own Marketing budget. The teams are expected to use that money – and a considerable amount of their lawyers' time (in office hours and out of office hours) to undertake "BD" activities to generate work *for their team.*

The outputs of that process can be curious. The firm's Employment Team, for example, could be targeting a company on a local business park, and would be writing to them, inviting them to events, sending them briefings and the like. And the Dispute Resolution Team could be writing to them as well. And the Real Estate Team. And the Corporate team. And the Debt Recovery Team.

Each team is promoting itself. And, of course, the selfish aim of each is to win a new case for their team – and I deliberately say a new "case for the team" rather than "a new client for the firm". The aim is mainly to win what I call Matter 1, or ".001", for a new client. Trumpets sound when that happens.

But it's hard work to win a new client if you lack powerful differentiators.

All Employment teams, for example, offer a retainer service with helplines and insurance-backed products. Any conversations with prospective clients can, therefore, gravitate towards price.

And whilst this is going on, there are lots of clients of the Employment Team in that firm for whom the Real Estate Team would love to act. And there are lots of clients of the Dispute Resolution Team for whom the Employment Team would love to act. And on it goes.

I do not believe that team-by-team marketing is the best way to grow a legal business in a sustainable way – a team might do well, but huge firm-wide opportunities are missed.

New brochures

Has your firm got cupboards full of brochures that the teams or the firm wanted, but which have not been used? Many a firm has.

There are two main things I would say about brochures. First, what's in them that sets your firm apart from other firms? Second, what is going to be done with the brochures? The main plan is usually to hand them out to prospective new clients. But if there isn't anything to differentiate you, their impact will be limited.

I tell the story later in this book about the superb corporate client who asked me (whilst he was beauty-parading my firm against two esteemed competitor law firms) why he, his family, and his company should use my firm. I said five words, and he said, "I'm all yours". My five words were, "Have a look at that", as I passed him a list of our powerful differentiators. It wasn't even in a posh brochure.

Also – to push another theme of this book at this early stage – do you really need new clients? I worked with a law firm that was very proud of its new, very expensive brochure. They had spent a lot of money and time on it.

I asked the Partners to put their hands up if they had 10 files in their office that they simply couldn't get around to working on. They all put their hand up. Is it me?

Achieving growth by opening up a new practise area

This is often tried, but it comes with risks. Many an exciting new venture has failed. The main risks are the cash impact, the risks to your reputation, your Professional Indemnity Insurance policy, and the Management time involved when you finally work out why that lawyer is no longer at their previous firm, and they were willing to move to a greenfield site and a start-up scenario.

Is there any certainty that the new lawyer will start bringing cash in quickly (i.e., don't just look at when they'll start sending bills out), and will that cash be more than you are paying them?

As it's a new area of law for your firm, who's going to monitor the quality and risk profile of their clients and of the lawyer's work and their delivery?

If a firm sets out on a mission to transform itself from a firm offering a narrow range of legal services to one offering "the full range of legal services", these issues are repeated – over and over again. "Sticking to your knitting" and staying with what you are best at is an extremely valid business strategy – and your chances of enjoying the real differentiator of being "the best" are higher than they might be if you are made up of a series of bolt-on lawyers from disparate legal backgrounds.

Opening a new office

I did this, and I like it as a growth strategy. I often see firms where the current owners have inherited a strange mix of offices in various locations.

"We wouldn't have an office there if we were starting the firm now", I often hear. When you understand the firm's evolution, these offices can be easily understood, but time moves on, and the reasons for having those offices may have gone. Some offices may no longer fit the aspirations, work-types, or strategy of the current owners. It is then for the firm to make hard decisions to reshape the firm, first by closing offices and secondly by opening new ones in relevant locations.

When it comes to opening a new office in a new town or city, the obvious options are (a) to go into that new location "cold", with your own new office and your own people – one of your lawyers who lives there perhaps, or (b) to bring in a local "star" lawyer or lawyers who'll open doors for you in that new location – which is how I did it – or (c) to acquire or merge with an established firm in that location.

Going back to the example I gave of the two companies that make cars, you might have Company A and Company B both making cars in a city, with no differentiators to boost either and nothing really between them, and now Company C has joined the fray (i.e., a new law firm comes into the local marketplace). If Company C doesn't have any differentiators either, how on earth will it break into the market presently serviced by Company A and Company B? Doesn't the arrival of Company C just increase the downward pressure on prices for all three businesses?

Across the UK, you can see examples of large, rich firms who have set up new operations in all the largest cities, but who do not seem to be offering anything in terms of differentiators to the clients they aspire to attract in the new regions. Their boasts are limited to those in the list of typical "differentiators" I talk about later – boasts such as "We're a Legal 500 firm" or "We're a Top 100 law firm". From what I can see, in reality the only differentiators they offer are not to *clients,* they are opportunities and higher salaries they extend to recruit local lawyers from the established local firms.

The task of winning clients to bolster the success of the new office at a time when you have nothing material to differentiate yourself from the firms that have been there for decades is just one challenge here. Managing people and offices at a distance is another, maintaining the cultural integrity of your firm another, risk management another, and the sudden and huge outflow of your cash is yet another.

My work with law firms with growth aspirations often starts with their desire to "have more locations" but it quickly morphs into us working together to get them "battle-ready" so they can later roll out a much stronger business model into new territories. I urge them to hold off from entering new markets until they look more like The Perfect Legal Business (in all the ways that this book explores) and only then to "press the button". When they do press the button, though, the risks are profoundly lower, and the prospects of success are profoundly higher.

Imagine if, as a law firm, you had real differentiators that would make clients choose you, whatever your prices, as well as make local lawyers choose you as their employer. You'd be able to go into all those towns and cities and trump the status quo that clients and lawyers there had become used to.

It would be like Company C arriving in a new town and shouting, "Our cars never break down".

Achieving growth by merging with local competitors

I am not talking here about the various large, well-funded businesses currently undertaking a programme of acquiring other law firms. Rather, I am referring, for example, to two (or more) firms in a town or city who decide to throw their lot in together after decades of competing against each other.

I once received a call from the Managing Partner of a competitor firm. Verbatim, the call went like this:

Him: "It's time you brought your firm into mine, Simon."

Me: "Why?"

Him: "Well, if you do, we'll have a turnover of £50 million."

Me: "I asked why?"

Him: "Simon – you're not listening!"

Being big is not a sound and effective strategy. I'd be very wary of bringing two firms together as a co-operation in a town or city to achieve growth. If you add one firm with no differentiators to another firm with no differentiators, and add cultural and behavioural differences and a host of fudges to make sure no one felt left out of ownership or management, you won't always create a growth beast – more like a monster. Examples abound of mergers where, decades later, you can still see the two groups of Partners. The position is only worsened when some profit-sharing formula had to be applied in order to give the owners of the more profitable of the two firms enhanced earnings.

These things can work, but sometimes they don't. Just saying.

Achieving growth by increasing prices

A lack of what I call "pride in pricing" is very evident as I travel around law firms. It is one of the many mistakes I made as a Managing Partner. Lawyers of all levels across my firm were responsible for their own pricing, and we had no collective confidence in pricing our services at a level commensurate with what we were offering. We truly had a great team delivering a great service – every lawyer, every time – and I don't think, with hindsight, that we charged enough for that.

Knowing what I know now, I believe it perfectly fair to charge a high price – for a great service. If a client doesn't want to pay that price, they are free to choose another firm. The better the service (in terms of both legal expertise and delivery of that expertise), the higher the price should be.

What some firms do, though, is just try to raise their prices without raising their game. Raising prices gets you more money per case for a while, but I have seen it leave various deep-rooted problems unaddressed, such as:

- Staff might still be leaving in droves

- The firm might be unable to attract new talent

- There might still be paralysis (or division) at Management level

- Client service levels could still be poor

- Partner behaviours might remain unaddressed

- Cross-selling and cross-caring to clients remains a missed opportunity

- On its own, "We're dearer" isn't a differentiator that your Marketing team can use

Higher prices are not, in themselves, a formula for sustained success. I worked for a while with a firm whose boast was that they were the dearest in their city. They couldn't explain why they were dearest – they couldn't justify their high prices with any compelling differentiators. In fact, in some places, their service levels were downright awful. Their business was struggling. Raising prices is not a panacea.

Summary of the "usual" growth options

Accepting that The Perfect Legal Business has to grow both profit and cash to remain perfect, we have cantered around the various common trails that law firms blaze in pursuit of that growth.

I hope I have been able to demonstrate that many of the most popular freeways to growth are pitted with potholes. They come with cost, risk, and uncertainty.

The Perfect Legal Business does none of these things – yet. It recognises that there are far better, cheaper, effective, local, sustainable, attainable, profitable, and cash-rich ways of securing the necessary growth.

Instead of looking outwards, The Perfect Legal Business starts by looking inwards – looking at itself, to get the foundations in place that will serve it very, very well in due course, when it does start looking outwards.

All too often, in rolling its business model out, a law firm is rolling out a flawed model – and the very success of that rolling out will bring the law firm pain rather than pleasure.

I was guilty of this – under my drive and direction, we rolled out a business model that was hugely successful on some levels. It had powerful differentiators, we had no shortage of clients and work, and we had no shortage of "top drawer" talent in our legal and Business Support teams. We delivered a great service – every lawyer, every time – and we got more and more work from our many existing and new clients.

But that's not enough if you are to be The Perfect Legal Business. The more we rolled out our "successful" model, the higher the pressures on our business. I was not alone in being guilty of this sin then, and I am not alone now.

Let's now take what we did right, and what we did wrong but which I have seen done right at successful firms and which I have since helped other firms to do right. In doing so, we can start to piece together the jigsaw pieces that will lay bare The Perfect Legal Business.

CHAPTER 7

WHAT THE PERFECT LEGAL BUSINESS DOES

Before the Perfect Legal Business shouts about itself in the many forms and in the many forums where that shouting can take place, it builds qualitative differentiators that make it stand out to clients in a crowded marketplace.

It develops, and then delivers on, what we might call "The PLB Way".

One of the two best business stories I have ever heard rammed home the importance of differentiators to me. Credit for the story goes to a BBC "Business Programme" presenter who told the story to a business audience at an event I attended in Reading a few years ago.

He was strolling one evening along the Keys in Florida, and saw a series of rickety, wooden stalls from which various people were selling freshly-caught lobsters. All the stalls still had lobsters on them and the stall-holders were chatting amongst themselves. All the stalls, that is, except one – he was packing up to go home. The speaker was intrigued, and he approached the stall-holder:

"You're all sold out?"

"Yup."

"Same lobsters as the others?"

"Yup."

"From the same boat?"

"Yup."

"And the same price as the other stalls?"

"Yup."

"So, why are you sold out and they're not?"

"Check this out" – at which point the stall-holder lifted the blackboard that had been on his stall all day. It read:

HAVE YOU TRIED LOBSTER IN LEMON?

BAKE THE LOBSTER FOR 2 HOURS,
WITH 4 SLICED LEMONS.

FREE LEMONS WITH ALL MY LOBSTERS.

The BBC speaker turned to the audience of businessmen and businesswomen and calmly asked, "Ladies and gentlemen – where are *your* lemons?"

No lemons – no standing out from the crowd. The lemons cost him 5 cents each, but they were a knockout differentiator in that particular marketplace.

The Perfect Legal Business embraces this approach. It designs and engineers substantive, meaningful differentiators. And saying you have differentiators is one thing – delivering on them constantly is another.

Having designed and engineered differentiators, the Perfect Legal Business commits itself to delivering on them consistently.

Thus, it effectively makes a promise to the external world. This is the essence of a *brand*. A brand is a promise. People buy brands, and people stay with brands. People don't question the price of brands.

Let's look at the "differentiators" that law firms typically use. They are what law firms currently say *their* lemons are; lemons that help them to stand out in a crowded marketplace.

Common law firm "differentiators" (as seen on their websites)

- We're unlike any other law firm [I couldn't see why]

- We're a law firm like no other [Again, I couldn't see why]

- We offer an excellent service [Really? So you have no files sitting on desks for weeks waiting?]

- Award-winning [So what – will your lawyers push my case and return my calls?]

- Honest [I should think so!]

- Expert [I should hope so!]

- Lawyers you can trust [again – I should hope so]

- Friendly [I've got enough friends – I want a good *lawyer*]

- We try to secure the best result for you [I should think so!]

- We work actively for you [I would hope so, at those prices]

- We opened in 1846 [I bet some of you were at the opening event]

- Tailored legal services [Tailored? I bet you still do it all your way!]

- We're a Top 100 firm [So only 99 other firms like you?]

- We're a Legal 500 firm [So only 499 other firms like you!?]

Are any of the above differentiators? No – not at all. It is genuinely very, very hard to find anything at all when looking at law firm websites that is truly a differentiator.

The success that is still there to be had, and the profit and cash that can still be generated, and the power to do something amazing for clients as a law firm looking after the biggest thing in clients' lives, are all still up for grabs. It is an amazing opportunity.

I can further demonstrate the power of differentiators with my other favourite business story – a story about my firm, which I touched upon in Chapter 6. In my firm, I believe we created some real differentiators. This was an area where we excelled (this book also references areas where I did not excel!).

One lunchtime, my direct line rang. It was the CEO of a lovely company – someone I came to know as a very sophisticated and seasoned buyer of legal services. His current lawyer was retiring, and he wanted to choose a new and more local law firm to look after him, his business, and his family. He had set up appointments to interview two larger local firms and asked if I wanted to be the third firm he would look at. I told him I'd be very interested, and I was given the last slot of his day.

He'd seen the first two firms by the time he came to me. On sitting down, he put his head in his hands and said, "Don't tell me anything about how long your firm's been around, about client-focused solutions, or about Partner-led teams. Just tell me why I should use you".

I said just five words.

He replied, "I'm all yours".

My five words? "Have a look at this", as I passed him a list of the differentiators we had engineered. That's the power of differentiators. He didn't even ask about our charges.

Just as powerful and telling was the conversation I had with the same CEO a year later, by which time we had carried out a wide range of legal work for him, his business, and his family.

Over a beer, I commented that we'd won his work with just five words. Being the sophisticated businessman he was, he replied, "No, you didn't. You won the *first case* with five words. You won all the rest because of *four words.*"

The five words (referring to our differentiators) and the four words – which we will discuss later – are aspects that we got very right. They are hugely significant aspects of The Perfect Legal Business, and when these work in tandem with the other pieces of The Perfect Legal Business jigsaw, they produce an incredible result where everyone is a winner.

Whilst I was Managing Partner, I had lunch with the Managing Partner of a competitor (and far more illustrious) law firm. I asked the Managing Partner in question why a client should use their firm. The Managing Partner looked at me for a long time, puzzled, in total silence. My comment to them was, "If you can't tell me why a client should use your firm, how can your people be expected to be out there marketing and developing business for you?".

Their reply was, "Go on then – why should anyone use *your* firm?" I answered immediately, "Because we offer every area of law and we deliver a great service – every lawyer, every time, guaranteed".

Knockout. And every one of our 200 or so people would have given – and believed in – the exact same answer.

"A great service – every lawyer, every time" was, therefore, our *first* differentiator. And we lived it.

"Service" as a differentiator warrants further investigation, so that's where we'll go next.

CHAPTER 8

SERVICE – THE GREATEST DIFFERENTIATOR

If the list of law firms' website "differentiators" above is the best that a law firm has in its armoury, then almost certainly their Marketing and Business Development initiatives (that can be hugely expensive in time and money) will not have anything like the desired effect or deliver anything like the required Return on Investment in the required timescale.

If only those efforts were boosted by the firm having real differentiators it could boast about. But what differentiators could there be?

First – here's a challenge to lawyers reading this. Complete this sentence as if you were personally sat in front of a potential client:

"You should use *me* because…"

Words that would be powerful here include "I'm simply the best in this area of law", or "This is all I do – there isn't anything I haven't seen and solved", or "What you'll get is my personal approach to looking after clients. I'll always push your case, and I'll always tell you where things are up to".

That's all quite compelling, though with the best will in the world, that lawyer may not be able to always push the case if they have a full caseload (namely, files on their desk that they can't get around to dealing with, and little in the way of support from good junior lawyers).

Next – can I ask the lawyers reading this to complete the following sentence as if they were sat in front of a potential client, or as if they were talking with a potential client at a networking event, where the client – a business client, say – has a broad range of legal needs:

"You should use my firm for all your legal needs because…".

It's a different challenge now, isn't it? Is the lawyer really going to say, "You should use my firm for all your legal needs because all my colleagues across all our teams are the best in their fields"? Or "because all my colleagues will always push your case and will always tell you where your case is up to"? Lawyers – with the best will in the world – can fall short on both these fronts, so how can the lawyer say that none of their colleagues will commit either of these sins?

So, it's difficult, yes, but not impossible, to have *firm-wide* differentiators that are far more effective than any of the commonly used "differentiators" listed above. I can think of three powerful differentiators that would make a client say "I'm all yours", like the discerning client I mentioned earlier said to me.

First – "I am the best". For many individuals, families, or businesses in complex legal situations, engaging a lawyer who is known as "the best" in that field is a "must", no matter the price. It is up to the lawyer whether they want to charge a premium price because they are "the best". Being "the best" is a superb differentiator – everyone else is an also-ran.

In this vein, I recall that when we procured a new Practise Management System for my firm, we were presented with a voluminous, opaque contract by the supplier. I wanted to know what that contract said both in letter and in spirit, so I researched who the best lawyer in the region was for advising on and negotiating IT contracts. I contacted him and he explained that he charged £10,000 plus VAT – before he'd even seen the contract. That's a ridiculous price, but from our conversation and my research, it was clear that he was indeed superb at this stuff, and he turned out to be invaluable. The fee paled against the value he added. That's the power of being known as "the best" – it's a real differentiator. He converted me from an enquiry into a client, and he named the price!

The second powerful differentiator I can think of as being attention-grabbing when heard or seen by clients would be a law firm that boasts, "We're the cheapest".

As a client "in the know", I might run a mile from a firm that said that. There's no way they could be "the cheapest" and still have great and senior lawyers doing the lead work on cases. I have seen many times how even simple legal issues have the power to explode in complexity, and I'd always want a good, experienced, lawyer on my case – not a junior lawyer who had a more experienced manager who waded in when something hit the buffers.

That brings me to only the third real differentiator I can think of. To my mind, it is *the* differentiator, par excellence. It is a game-changer in so many ways and is a foundation of The Perfect Legal Business and, therefore, of this book.

It is the ability of a law firm to *genuinely* make the boast that I have already hinted at – "We deliver a great service – every lawyer, every time". That is, literally *every* lawyer, *every* time.

"A great service – every lawyer, every time" was our whole strategy. We all knew it, believed in it, and were proud of it. For us, this was not a hollow boast but rather something in which we invested a lot of time, money, passion, courage, determination, and technology.

"Service". The very word is more complicated in this forum than you might at first think. When it comes to lawyers, "good service" consists of a host of aspects:

- Legal technical knowledge – it's not much of a service if the lawyer doesn't know the law

- Framing that technical knowledge into practical, understandable, real-life, sensible options

- Communicating that advice and those options in a way that that client will understand

- Accepting that a client will get more out of you, and you out of them, by talking

- Being accessible and responsive when they do try to talk with you

- Doing all of this within a reasonable timescale

- Not running up costs on things that don't progress the case (see the "one unit" issue, below)

- Cheap work being done by cheap lawyers

- Essentially, always pushing the case, and always telling the client

- Making the client feel better, not worse

It's effectively all about "Push & Tell". If you do that – every lawyer, every time – you'd avoid the most frequent complaints that are made about law firms' service levels.

You'd also have an extremely valuable differentiator and an ever-expanding list of clients, all of whom would join your sales force. All too often, though, as you will have seen from research over the years, what clients get is not the "Push & Tell" treatment but the "Black Hole" treatment. Sometimes, the case is pushed; sometimes, it isn't. Sometimes, whether the case is pushed or not, the client isn't told. Being a client and not knowing where your case is up to is a horrible feeling. You'll know that well if you've been there.

Clients suffer because their file sits on the desk of a very busy lawyer who simply never gets around to working on it. Or because they call and call their solicitor but never get a call back. (If you have never been the client engaged in a hugely emotive and important case, you will have no idea what it is like waiting for a call, not getting a call, and then not getting your own calls returned. It is truly sickening.)

What is good service to a lawyer, though, is not always good service from a client's perspective. Consider a lawyer who works all night drafting complex documents for a corporate client and who emails hundreds of pages of re-drafts to the client at 5 am with an email saying, "Latest drafts attached – comments?".

To the lawyer, that may feel like amazing service – "I worked until 5 am!" To the client, that is a nightmare. They're trying to run a business.

Or the Private Client lawyer who spends weeks (and lots of chargeable hours) crafting a thesis that analyses a complex legal situation, which gets sent to a client weeks or months later, and which leaves the "man-in-the-street" client staring at a long letter wondering what it's about and with a hundred questions.

In assessing whether a lawyer is delivering a great service and making the clients feel better rather than worse, I always apply what I call the "Mum and Dad" test. My Mum and Dad are very bright and can understand nearly everything, but watching them try to understand letters they'd received from their *own* solicitors was painful. Many a lawyer I have worked with has had letters that I found on the printer thrust back at them with the comment, "My Mum and Dad wouldn't have a clue what that letter was saying".

Of course, you never see law firms saying, "Our service is dreadful". On the contrary, "Great Service" is a regular law firm boast. But I simply do not believe that many firms can deliver on a promise that "we will always deliver a great service". Across all my dealings in my personal, family, wider family, and business lives, I've never come across a *firm* that gets over this high bar. Individual lawyers *sometimes* can, but never a whole firm.

It is usually an empty boast, but it is empty for entirely understandable reasons. It may be that a client could use Lawyer A in a firm, and the service on that occasion could be great.

That might lead the client to use Lawyer A again if the same expertise is needed later. But Lawyer A might be busier by then. They might be ill. They might be on holiday. They might be tied up in a big case for weeks, unable to give real attention to anything else. For whatever reason, unless *the team and the firm* has systems and monitoring and resources in place to make sure that whatever is going on in the business (and personal) life of Lawyer A, clients will not be kept waiting for weeks, then the firm cannot boast that they always provide a great service.

My point here is that on their own, with the best will in the world, Lawyer A simply *cannot* deliver on a promise that he or she will always deliver a great service. It is not just *their* problem – it is the *firm's* challenge. The firm cannot bark at lawyers and say, "You've always got to deliver a knockout service" – it's simply not possible. A team and an all-firm commitment is what is needed.

This challenge becomes even clearer if the client is so impressed with Lawyer A (who is, say, dealing with Matter .001 for a new client), that the client approaches Lawyer A with a different type of case they need help with. As it's outside Lawyer A's expertise, they have to pass it to Lawyer B in another team, who opens up Matter .002 for that client. (By the by, *that's* what I call marketing).

71

But is any system, protocol, commitment, training, reward, team effort, monitoring, management, or accountability structure in place to ensure that the lawyers in different teams deliver a great service so that the client gets a great service there, too, and a great service is delivered – every lawyer, every team, every time? It's only if that all exists that the client will keep coming back so that they clock up more and more matters with the firm, taking their Client Matter Printout up to .003, .004, .005, .006, .007, and beyond.

These things are not usually in place. Many of the boasts that are made by firms around "service" would not stand up to even the simplest form of scrutiny.

Scrutiny such as "Okay – you say your service levels are always excellent. Tell me how you ensure that lawyers in your Employment Team, your Property team, and your Litigation team, all deliver a great service, regardless of what the lawyers have on their desks?" There are not many law firms that can give compelling answers to this question.

History is littered with examples of one particular lawyer impressing a client so that the client brought more work-types to the firm, only for lawyers in other teams to fail to ring the client back, or to bill the life out of the job, or to put the file into storage.

Law firms may say, "We check inactivity reports, so we know when a file has not been worked on". Maybe, but all that has to happen for a file not to appear on an inactivity report is a lawyer spending one unit on it. One unit will rarely take a case far, and all the while, the client is sat waiting for progress at a time when all looks well from the firm's perspective.

(It's an incomplete solution, but at a minimum, it might be better to tailor your inactivity reports so that they report on files that have not had at least one hour spent on them in the last month. A month is an incredibly long time in the life of a client with a matter that is of huge importance to them.)

So, what can be done to build up a meaningful, high-quality, sustainable, service-based differentiator for a law firm?

The first thing I do with law firms is work with them to design a Service Pledge that suits them and their personality, and on which they feel sure they can all deliver, all the time. Sometimes, this begins with a short and simple set of promises which can be developed further over time. The main thing is to arrive at a promise that the *whole firm* will *absolutely keep*.

We do this by getting the whole firm (for it is the whole firm, not just the lawyers, that deliver the service) to look at what makes good service and what makes bad service – *from a client's perspective*. I do this by giving groups (made up of a mix of legal and Business Support staff) an imaginary scenario where I – as a client – am in an urgent, complex, difficult position.

Dividing each group into two imaginary law firms, I ask one "firm" – Bad & Co – to explain what they will do to turn my already difficult position into an absolute catastrophe for me. I ask the other "firm" – Good & Co – to describe how they will move heaven and earth to get me through the predicament and to a sound solution. Starting with Bad & Co, we map out what evil works they come up with:

BAD & CO	GOOD & CO (Just insert the opposite!)
Take the urgent, complex case on, even though it's not something you've done much of	
Pass the file to a junior, unsupervised lawyer	
Don't communicate with the client	
Don't keep the client updated	
Don't acknowledge receipt of anything	
Don't return the client's calls	
Don't stick to deadlines or agreed timings	
Work on other files that are more urgent	
Only work on this file when you have to	
Never really get into the detail	
Tell the client it'll cost £5,000 and bill £10,000	
Pass the file between lawyers so they all have	

BAD & CO	GOOD & CO (Just insert the opposite!)
to read into it, and they all record their time	

The amazing thing is that if you look at what the teams at Bad & Co usually come up with, when asked to do their very worst for a client-in-need, they come up with things that clients actually complain of!

Many of them are things I have personally experienced over the years, and many people with whom I have talked have also experienced them.

From this, you can see that it's not hard to arrive at a series of simple promises to clients about what you will do, and what you will not do, when you deal with any case for them. Thus, you can arrive at a Service Pledge that your whole firm has designed (with their heads and hearts) and that all of your people believe in. You will arrive at a Service Pledge that prospective clients will very much like the sound of (because they've often had bad experiences with lawyers in the past), and which will mean existing clients stay with you and use you for more and more legal work – without looking at the price.

Going back to the client who instructed my firm on the basis of me simply saying, "Have a look at that" (where "that" was our list of differentiators), that client grew into a large client that gave work to a good number of teams across my firm. You will recall that when I mentioned to him (a year down the road) that we'd won his work with just five words, his canny reply was that we'd only won the first case (or the first chance) with those five words, and all the other cases had been won because of *four* words.

The four words – verbatim – were "You give a shit".

He explained that every lawyer he dealt with at my firm delivered exceptional service. There was a clear "way" that we *all* did things. He said that everyone he had dealt with at my firm delivered the same great service and that during a lifetime of using lawyers around the world as part of his business, he had never seen anything like it before. He said that it was clearly no accident. He said that he was no longer bothered about the price and that everyone he ever referred to us reported the same phenomena back to him.

The second "internal" thing that's needed to enable a firm to really deliver a great service – every lawyer, every time – is a team ethos where everyone is empowered (indeed *proud*) to put their hands up whenever they feel they are not delivering on the firm's Service Pledge. Them putting their hands up in this way – to their line manager – is to be celebrated, and the challenge is passed up the line until a solution to the challenge is found. Where this breaks down is where a lawyer cannot get around to working on all the files that they have and they do not feel comfortable putting their hand up in this way, or they want to keep all the files so they can hit their individual billing target. Or they put their hands up and nothing happens. Whatever the reason for files not being worked on, that is not a different, differentiating way of working.

The third "internal" thing that is needed here is a commitment by Management that the firm's resources will be applied to encourage the entire firm to work to this Service Pledge (i.e., this brand).

Embracing and delivering on the Service Pledge should be key factors in the appraisal process and, of course, the induction process. Anyone who helps the firm as a whole to deliver on the Pledge or to build an even stronger Pledge, should be seen as someone as valuable if not more valuable than a good biller. And anyone (whoever they are) who does not buy into the Service Pledge and who continues to exhibit non-Pledge behaviours (which could be as simple as never returning calls) must be seen as someone who is undermining your whole brand. And the Partners in the firm have to lead by example. If they turn a blind eye, how can you expect people under them to work to build your brand and the value of your business?

The fourth internal thing that is needed is teamwork and delegation. Good lawyers at good firms are always busy. They'll never have an empty desk, so they'll never be able to give a new case their full time and attention. Or they will, but other files will get pushed aside.

But there is a way to achieve consistent service excellence and to deliver on your brand in a way that makes profit... however many files come in.

Consider the position of senior Lawyer A who charges, say, £300 an hour and who works as an island with no support from any junior lawyers. Let's say that he or she usually does five chargeable hours a day (that's high! There's much more on chargeable hours and Utilisation below).

If a new file comes to Lawyer A – perhaps as a result of the firm's marketing activity and spend – then unless

Lawyer A starts doing, say, 7 chargeable hours a day, there's going to be no financial gain to the firm of that new case coming in. What might happen is that Lawyer A will push the current case they're working on to the back of the desk, and they'll start working on the new case instead. The firm was earning £300 an hour, and now, having got a great new case, it is still earning, well, £300 an hour. And one happy client is now shortly going to become an unhappy client – along with all the others that are already at the back of the desk. There is simply no way Lawyer A can deliver on a Service Pledge to always "Push & Tell".

Now consider Lawyer B at The Perfect Legal Business. At this firm, each lawyer has support from junior lawyers. Crucially – they have support from *good* junior lawyers they can *trust*. Suitably trained in the art of delegation, Lawyer B's focus is on getting the current file into a position when a lieutenant lawyer can take it over, under B's ongoing supervision. Lawyer B charges £300 for their senior expertise, and the lieutenant charges £200 for theirs. The firm is now earning £500 an hour, as Lawyer B isn't working on that file now – they're earning their £300 an hour on another client's file.

The client benefits in two ways – their case is still being pushed, and junior work is being done at a junior rate. That brings both service excellence and value for money. There is a huge gulf between the experience of a client using Lawyer A and that of the client using Lawyer B. And the latter's firm is making far more money.

Externally, too, there is something you can do which not only advertises the fact that there is something different about your firm and that the difference is quality of service, but it also allows you to ensure that you are actually delivering on your brand at all times. You need real-time client feedback and quality control.

Do you ask your clients for feedback on your services? Some firms (or often it's a case of some lawyers, in some teams, at some firms) send a questionnaire out to some clients at the end of some cases, or the end of the year. I have seen other firms that are far more military and thorough about it where every client gets a questionnaire at the end of every case, across the firm.

Having committed ourselves to delivering "A great service – every lawyer, every time", we wanted to go further than this at my firm. We wanted to know that we were actually delivering a great service *as the case progressed*. It wasn't enough for us to find out that the client hadn't been happy at the end of a case. We wanted *real-time* quality control and brand measurement.

We could have done this manually and in a labour-intensive way (at the time, no software existed that made this easy or indeed possible). Our superb IT team, though, came to the rescue in designing and building the "ABC Text" system we launched.

Every time a file was opened for any client, we explained to them our commitment to delivering a great service – every lawyer, every time – and we asked them if they'd work with us to make sure we delivered on that promise. At intervals that the client chose during their case (weekly, fortnightly, monthly, or quarterly), our system automatically sent them a text simply asking if our service was A (Great) or B (Okay) or C (Poor).

If anyone replied with a "C", I as Managing Partner, would ring them.

I rang a few such clients and the impact was always the same – astonishment that anything at all came from their replies, let alone a call from the Managing Partner. Unhappy clients became not just happy clients, but amazed, loyal, evangelical clients.

The results were gathered centrally and shared internally. The results were also published on the homepage of our website. That's brave!

The point here is that in law firms (usually law firms looking to grow but not sure how to go about it), there are nearly always files that need good time spent on them – one hour rather than one unit. The client would benefit, and the business would benefit, if all files that needed such time got it.

And while we're on "one unit", consider the impact on a client's case and a client's bills of the "one unit" system. It can be devastating.

One unit can be very valuable – a key (short) letter, for example. Having been a law firm client many times, though, "one unit" is rarely very valuable – particularly when several people spend "one unit" discussing the file and they all record the time. As a client, when you ask for a time printout, and you see how high cost levels have been run up, it is often a build-up of "one units" by one or more people. There is often ample justification for a client to question the value for money they have received in such cases. The costs shoot up while the file goes nowhere. Another benefit, therefore, of lawyers being able to work on files when they need good time investing in them is that whilst the bills may be no lower – and may indeed be higher – there is *material progress* on the file and, therefore, the client sees value for money.

In short, having been on the thick end of poor service from law firms, it seems to me that "Management" is often happy to boast about "excellent service" but hasn't thought about what is needed to make sure that their firm delivers on that promise when it comes to the level at which it really counts – the granular level.

To jump out of the legal sector once more to reinforce my point, it's like a restaurant owner who spends a fortune building a great venue, hiring a top chef, designing a stunning menu, making a lot of noise, who wins awards and goes mad on social media – and then doesn't have enough waiters and waitresses on the floor who have had the right "customer experience" training. What happens? There is no warm welcome for customers, they wait ages to even get a drink, they start feeling bad about the night instead of good, the food is slow and cold, and they don't know who's looking after them. They might even have trouble paying at the end of the night.

On paper, the food should be amazing, and the whole restaurant venue, too, but the overall experience is poor. I've been to restaurants like this and I know how I talk of them after the event – I certainly don't join what should be their ever-growing sales team. I've had the same experience with law firms.

Most adults have used a lawyer, but not many have *got* a lawyer. This is why. The technical law is rarely lacking, but the "client experience" often is.

I believe that this whole question of "service" is critical to The Perfect Legal Business, as this is the key to building a true legal *brand*, to creating a real differentiator, to developing clients, to earning a lifetime's value out of them (and their families and friends), to getting your clients to do your marketing for you, to boosting the effectiveness of your own marketing, to growing your profitability and your cash reserves, and to being a legal business that you and your people can be absolutely proud of.

Pride is not a sentiment that all law firms engender or seek or enjoy. All too often, I have spoken with lawyers who are not proud of what they themselves do – they're simply too busy to give clients a good, proactive service – or of what their colleagues do (some lawyers would still rather send a client to another firm than to their colleague down the corridor whose service they simply don't trust).

I have seen it so many times – growth comes (and client satisfaction and loyalty increase) when a firm gets more lawyers in, not more cases. I have seen teams and firms that I have been in (and teams and firms that I have worked with) grow without a single extra case coming in, where more lawyers are recruited, cases are distributed, and individual caseloads go down.

Spending more time on fewer cases, where lawyers can all deliver on a firm's Service Pledge, where more time is spent on each file, more time is captured, and less time is lost by lawyers dashing from file to file to file, is good for everyone – in the short term and the long term.

In The Perfect Legal Business, service, profit, cash, and growth are close bed-fellows.

CHAPTER 9

CLIENT SELECTION AND ENGAGEMENT

The Perfect Legal Business is fussy about who it takes on as clients – for a host of reasons. With clients come risks – reputational risks, risks of losing money on the case, and risks of claims against your Professional Indemnity policy.

There's another risk, too – the risk that in adding to an already great number of clients, you won't be looking after any of them in a way that would make your service a powerful differentiator or in a way that would help you to wring a lifetime's value out of each client.

Not only does The Perfect Legal Business know that the more clients you have, the more client issues you'll get (many of which will take considerable Management time to put to bed), but it also knows that more and more clients and more and more files (to which more and more compliance gets attached) will need more and more desks and IT equipment and a growing Business Support team.

Having lots of files makes you very busy, and on paper, more files should mean more profit, which justifies the increased spending across the firm. Often, though, lawyers and firms are simply too busy to make as much money as they should. Why do busy lawyers typically only record 4-5 chargeable hours a day, even though they're often in the office for far more hours than that? One answer is that they are running from pillar to post and aren't catching all the time they spend on their many files.

And what kind of service are they providing as they run from pillar to post, and as surplus files sit on the desk with even committed lawyers unable to deal with them?

When I was a fee-earner, I had personal experience of passing a high number of my files to other lawyers in my team – I had put my hand up because I had far too many files – and I was no less busy as a result. The files I retained started getting a much better service. I have lost count of the number of times when I have seen a new lawyer come into a team, be given cases that the existing lawyers were "working on" (or rather, "had in storage"), everyone remained busy throughout, and billing and client satisfaction went up – with no new cases coming in.

To make sure the clients get the service they want, and to make sure the firm generates maximum profit and cash, the key is not "thousands of files". There are two other keys, instead.

First, you need to ensure that individual lawyers don't have more cases than they can deal with under their full-time, sole stewardship. This can be achieved by having more lawyers and spreading the cases around. It can also be achieved by having a model where senior lawyers have good and trusted junior lawyer support, and they are charged with "filling the vessels" of their supporting lawyers and supervising their work on an ongoing basis.

The second key is to ensure that the firm simply does not take on all the cases that come knocking on its door, by setting a number of rules, or bars, that every case and client has to get over. In short, I am now an advocate of filtering out some cases and clients so that a firm can do less but better.

Rule 1 – Is this case in an area of law where we have real expertise?

Many a Professional Negligence claim against a law firm has arisen as a result of a lawyer or law firm "dabbling". If you are not steeped in a particular work-type and you come up against a lawyer who is, you (and your client) are at real risk.

When I was a Commercial Litigation solicitor, even I saw on many occasions how a detailed knowledge of the White Book gave me and my client a distinct advantage over general practitioners who didn't have the luxury of spending all their time with their heads in that book. That was before the advent of the legion of online resources that are now available – it can only have got much worse now. Be brave and say no – and I don't mean even where there's a big fee up for grabs. I mean *particularly* where there's a big fee up for grabs. Just say no.

There can be other benefits of taking such an approach. I recall an AIM-listed corporate client for whom I was the Client Partner and with whom we'd built up a great relationship where we got all their "bread and butter" work, but not their "Listed" work, as they used a City firm for that. One day, they asked me if we could act for them in a large corporate acquisition. In conjunction with our Corporate team, who were strongly of the view that we did not have the resources of a City firm (so could not take the case on), we told the client that they would be better served by their current lawyers on that job. The clients were bowled over by our honest, selfless response – it took the relationship to an even higher plane.

I once spent some quality time with an inspiring lawyer who could teach us all a good lesson. He had long been the typical busy lawyer taking on anything that came through his door. He was being run off his feet, was unable to deliver a service he was proud of, and he wasn't making anything like the money his activity and stress levels warranted.

He decided to focus on what he was best at, and to turn away every other work-type. He explained to me that all he did now was Residential Conveyancing, and he now sent all Matrimonial, Private Client, etc., work to a firm down the road. More than that, though, he did Conveyancing *at a high hourly rate* – no fixed-fee quotes for him.

We compared my firm's scale fees against some "actuals" that he had recently charged. His fees were over double ours. And he was busy. And clients referred clients to him. If they wanted a fixed price quote, he just told callers he didn't do them. Sounds amazing, doesn't it? But then he asked me this question: "How long have you been here this morning?"

Me: "About 40 minutes."

Him: "Have you heard the phone ring?"

Me: "No."

Him: "It never does – because I ring everyone. All the time. Every day. No one ever has to ring me. I push everyone, and I get conveyances completed quicker than clients have ever seen before. I stick to what I'm good at, my service is phenomenal, and I charge properly for it."

He was happier, more proud, making more money, and delivering a better service, than ever before.

Rule 2 – Don't compete on price

The second rule I now advocate is "We're dear". But that's not enough. If you can't justify *why* you're dearer than your competitors, why would someone pay more to use you? The Perfect Legal Business is able to say, "We're dear because we have real differentiators and they come at a price".

See the story about the conveyancer just above – he was able to say effectively, "I charge double what my competitors charge, but cast your mind back to the last house move you were involved in. Remember when no one called you back?

"Recall not knowing whether or when you were going to be moving and not knowing whether or when you should arrange the removal company for? Remember not having a clue where anything was up to or not understanding what any blockage was or how any blockage would be resolved? Remember pulling your hair out? You avoid all of that with me, but you've got to pay for it."

If a firm can embrace the service ethos in a concrete way so that the whole firm is geared up and committed to delivering a great service – every lawyer, every time – there is your ability to complete the above sentence. "We're dearer because you, the client, will benefit from our Service Pledge. It's on our website – have a look. We all work to it. It essentially means we *always* push your case and we *always* tell you where we are up to. We call it the *PLB Way*".

If the whole firm is delivering a great service, changing clients' lives for the better, every time, that is something that everyone in the firm can really be proud of – for it is an achievement indeed. Hand in hand with that pride ought to go pride in the value of what the whole firm is delivering, which should translate into what I call "Pride in Pricing". If you are doing something amazing, don't give it away. Don't charge Volkswagen prices for a Bentley-level service.

A Real Estate Partner at a firm I was working with said he was facing a "new client pricing" issue at that very moment. A developer had asked him how much he'd charge for (I think) a lease renewal. The Partner had replied, "£1,650". The client had replied that if the lawyer would do it for £850, the lawyer could have all his lease work. I asked the lawyer what his reply would have been if we hadn't been looking at the whole service and "Pride in Pricing" topic. He said he would have grabbed the developer's offer, and they would have celebrated winning "all his work".

And now?

The Partner went back to the developer and explained that he and this firm did things a certain way, delivering an excellent service and that the firm didn't want any of his work, let alone all of his work, if the price was £850. They won that job at £1,650 and the rest of his work, too, on the strength of the Partner's initial self-worth and the service he delivered in Matter .001.

Rule 3 – Define what you are doing (and what you are not doing) for the client

In short – define your retainer. There are two reasons for this. Firstly, the Professional Indemnity Insurance reason.

Many a PII insurer has paid out where a client suffered a loss and blamed the lawyer, only for the lawyer to be unable to show that dealing with *that* aspect was not his or her responsibility. Tax aspects of a property or corporate transaction have often been the culprit. Firms should have very detailed carve-out clauses limiting and clarifying what they are doing – and not doing – for the client.

The second reason is financial. If you set out what is in the (high) price and what isn't, everyone has clarity. "Mission creep" (doing more and more work within the initial price) is avoided, as is a surprise bill and, therefore, client unhappiness. The client should be told what you are doing, what the price is, and that any extra work will mean an extra price as you don't undertake any legal work without charging for it. Of course, the lawyer then has to be rigorous in looking out for "mission creep" and on raising this with the client when it arises.

Rule 4 – Clients have to pay you quickly

This brings us back to cash. Not "money", not "profit", but "cash". Nothing but cash can keep a firm going.

As well as having "Pride in Pricing", the lawyers at The Perfect Legal Business have a "Cash Commitment".

In 2017, when I was moving house a year or so after my law firm had been acquired, I came across the "bible" that the transaction had generated – all the data and all the printouts that were disclosed to the purchaser by us to give them a full picture of our business, warts and all.

By that time, I'd been out of private practise and out of the 100-mph "hot seat" of being Managing Partner for about a year. Peace had returned to my mind. I had clarity of thought.

In the chaos around me that comes with moving house, I sat down with my printouts and a cup of coffee, and I began to read.

Before I continue, let's pause to reflect on how various business models behave in "cash" terms. This will help us to see just how important "cash-positivity" is, as opposed to "cash-negativity". It pays (literally) to spend some time assessing where your firm (and each team within it) is on this cash spectrum – and for each of your teams, and indeed individual lawyers, to assess where they are on it.

At one extreme, you have businesses such as insurance companies who take your cash and might never give you anything in return. They invest that cash to try to make real profit out of it. That's cash-positive!

You also have businesses that, for example, sell gift vouchers or Christmas hampers – they have your money for a long time before they give anything in return for it. That's cash-positive, too.

Then you have the Amazon model, where they also get your money before they've given you anything. Typically, having got your money up front, businesses like this agree long credit terms with the people they have to pay – their suppliers. They can thus retain a fortune in cash in this way. Again, cash positive.

Then you have the "bricks and mortar" retail model, where you hand over your cash at the same time as you get what you are buying. That's cash-neutral, though if the retailer has the buying power, it will make sure its suppliers are on anything up to 120 days credit – so they're sat on a cash pile for a long time. Again, brutal cash positivity.

All of the above businesses are clear cash businesses. No cash? No supply to the customer. There is no cash at risk at all for them. They are hugely strong businesses in cash terms because they have made themselves cash-positive.

The opposite is to be cash-negative – where you use *your own* cash to effect the supply and then you have to try to recover payment from your client or customer. It's a very different ball game. Cash negativity brings cash risk, and it can kill.

Such businesses move away from being brutal cash businesses in the Amazon mould. They supply their goods or services *before* they are paid. Law firms typically fall into this bracket (though they don't always have to). It is a real question of trust now; they supply services *on credit*. They agree the time for payment with the client or customer prior to a contract being agreed (hopefully), and after the supply of the services they send the client an invoice, which hopefully the client will pay on time. Of course, clients don't all do that.

Within these credit businesses, there is another spectrum. At one extreme, you have a wide array of non-legal businesses – designers, printers, IT companies, stationery and office equipment companies, and so on. Typically, these businesses might not have the deepest of pockets, so they are very good at getting the cash in if you don't pay on time. They pass the case to their debt recovery company who get to work on it – they simply can't afford not to.

At the other extreme, you have law firms. You would not see many of the businesses just mentioned with a "Debtors" list that had so many columns on it – 0-30 days, 30-60 days, 60-90 days, 90-120 days, and 120 days+ columns are regular sights at law firms. Nor would you usually see numbers of the *size* you see on law firms' printouts in any "aged debt" columns at any other businesses. The "normal" businesses above would be horrified and completely perplexed that a business (particularly one with a cash appetite like that of a law firm) could allow so much of its cash to remain in its customers' pockets. What on earth could it be using to run the firm? The answer is often… the overdraft.

So, there I was with my printouts and my coffee, and I started to read. Despite what I recall as the incredible efforts of our Head of Credit Control, my printouts were no different to those of the dozens of law firms that I had seen and worked with over the decades. Our debtors reached across all those columns and the numbers were bigger than they should have been. And, of course, as well as paying all the lawyers' salaries and all the overheads (and as we were based in the UK), we were paying the VAT on the bills that hadn't been paid.

I could see that whilst we had done noble work that we could be proud of in relation to service levels (that is, work that favoured the client), I had not had the same focus on making our law firm more of a cash business (i.e., a focus which would have favoured my firm). Frankly, I didn't know what the options were other than to bark at everyone about getting money on account and setting up a robust and ever-shorter and more determined credit control system.

I think there's a spectrum of credit control approaches at law firms. At one end, you have the completely casual approach with no chasing going on at all. At the other extreme, you have the system we had – lots of regular chasing of the clients and the lawyers by a (brilliant) Credit Control executive. I now realise that's the wrong spectrum to be looking at.

It doesn't have to be that way, as the song goes. In The Perfect Legal Business, it is not like that at all. The Perfect Legal Business is a cash business as far as a law firm that supplies services on credit can be.

Instead of the payment terms being lost in a 16-page retainer letter, the time for payment is made very clear to clients by the lawyers at the outset. It's part of the lawyers' job and it's therefore part of the lawyers' opening discussion. "We can't work with clients who don't pay on time". Easy. Are you really going to take on a client who says in response, "Hey that's not fair – I'm not happy with that at all?"

Where your branding is clear and your differentiators are strong, where your "Pride in Pricing" and your "Cash Commitment" is high, your lawyers will feel perfectly fine in setting a high price, setting out narrow retainers, insisting on quick payment, insisting on cash on account, and in dealing with any late payers themselves rather than seeing them as someone else's problem – particularly if all of these things are part of the ongoing performance review and a lawyer's career development programme.

I have seen to dramatic effect positions in other law firms where it is not the lawyers' job to simply do billing. I have shown earlier in this book how mere billing can hurt your business, so in some firms (who have cracked this troublesome nut) it is the lawyers' clear job to *bring cash in, not to send bills out.*

Not only is it the lawyers' responsibility and they are accountable for it – and rewarded or something otherwise – but also the Pride in Pricing and the Cash Commitment on the part of their lawyers is such that they themselves are outraged if a client doesn't pay them on time. They personally – by working with Credit Control – take action to secure payment. Securing payment on time for a brilliantly provided service is a matter that is personal to every lawyer in The Perfect Legal Business.

The Perfect Legal Business thus moves from being a credit-ravaged business to being more of a cash business.

Any business that delivers its goods or services without a clear and certain timeline between supply and payment, will feel pain. I know.

Summary on Client Engagement

Having set these four rules in respect of new clients in addition to all AML and reputation-management requirements that you have in place, you can be more confident that clients who do satisfy your rules and who do come on board will be good for your business – in the longer term as well as in the shorter term. Your ability to look after these good clients will not be undermined by you playing a "numbers" game, based on the view that the more clients you have, the better.

The Perfect Legal Business attracts clients with its stand-out brand, but like the bouncers at a popular night club there is then a strict code over who can actually come in. The Perfect Legal Business sets these very clear rules and it thus re-calibrates the balance of power between law firm and client in the correct way. Some clients might be repelled at that stage, but The Perfect Legal Business has confidence that those clients are not right for it.

Now that the client has been attracted to the brand and has agreed the rules of the game, work on the client's case can begin. This moment is the acid test for the law firm, though; is its service going to be spectacularly normal or spectacularly different? The firm has to do a good job and deliver a great service – every lawyer, every time – if it is to not only keep that case and, therefore, that client but also do what The Perfect Legal Business always does. That is, to see the case not as a *case* but as a *client*, and to extend maximum care and secure a lifetime's value out of every good client, their family, and their business.

CHAPTER 10

KEEPING .001 (AND STARTING THE JOURNEY TOWARDS .007)

Imagine a healthy tree with a solid trunk and various branches coming off it. That represents your typical client. Each branch is an area of law in which a law firm might be able to extend some care to this personal or business client over the coming years.

Now, let's imagine that tree telephones a law firm with – say – an Employment issue. It is irrelevant here whether the client is a personal client or a corporate client. During the first call to the law firm, that tree/client will utter a single word that will have a huge impact. It will mention "Employment".

Immediately, it will be as if the tree has been put into a de-branching machine, so all that is left is one branch, and that branch will be sent through to the Employment team, where it will land on the desk of an Employment lawyer. The rest of the branches are effectively sawdust.

The client is immediately "owned" by the lawyer on whose desk the case lands. No one else in the firm may ever know about them.

If that lawyer has no "Pride in Pricing" and no "Cash Commitment", then it does not follow that this client is even going to help the firm grow its profit and cash reserves as it might.

If that lawyer already has a busy caseload, and is struggling to deal with all the files they have on their desk awaiting attention, they are going to be unable to deliver the kind of service that will keep this new client happy. Their service to other clients will also deteriorate.

The outcome might very well be that even if the lawyer can keep the case and get to the end of it, the firm won't make enough money on the case, won't get paid quickly enough, and the client really won't be back for more if any other legal need crops up.

This happens thousands of times – every adult and every businessman or businesswoman has *used* a lawyer, but not many *have* a lawyer.

And, all the while, the firm's Private Client Team, Property Team, Dispute Resolution Team, etc., are having meetings whilst *they* struggle to find new clients.

The Perfect Legal Business recognises the opportunity that the tree discussed above offers to its business. It doesn't see the branch as a branch, or the case as a case; rather, it sees the case as but the first opportunity to extend care to a client (i.e., to the whole tree over time). It sees a new client's Matter .001 not as a billing opportunity for one lawyer in one team, but as the first step in a long journey towards Matter .007 for that client and beyond. That journey leads to comfort and protection for the client, and it leads to sustained and easy profit, cash, and pride for the law firm. It also brings the client into your sales team.

So, what might The Perfect Legal Business do when it comes to engaging with a client? What can it do that is better than rival law firms who have fallen into the department-based method of client engagement, described above? What could it do that gets it off on an altogether different footing with every client?

Although (as will be clear from this book) the firm where I was Managing Partner was far from being anything like The Perfect Legal Business, this was another area where we showed courage and imagination (alongside our whole service ethos, differentiators, and brand-building), and where we saw real impact and success.

In my firm, clients didn't come into a department or team – they came into the centre. Into one of two schemes or "client clubs".

If they were individuals or families, they came into the central scheme or club that we set up for them. If they were a business client, they came into the business scheme or business club. We also tried to get owners of businesses to join the personal / family scheme – they're people after all, people with quite complex personal legal needs.

The engagement was central. No individual or team owned the client, as the commonwealth did. We all did. I recall, at one stage, we had some 20,000 people in the personal scheme and about 1,000 businesses in the corporate scheme. The whole messaging and engagement here was deeper than just the case that the client brought to us.

A small but large difference can be seen in the first letters that we sent out to new clients. Most firms write to the client saying, "Dear Mr. Smith, re your Employment case". Our letters began, "Dear Mr. Smith – welcome to the world of care that we offer to you and your family now and in the future".

The client of The Perfect Legal Business has to be owned by everyone. There is a central engagement and a universal commitment to looking after all clients in *The PLB Way* that will benefit clients and all colleagues, not just a particular lawyer's own billing target. It's not about billing, and it's not about selling. It's about caring and it's about pride. The money will follow.

These schemes and clubs came with a range of benefits for the clients. Not least, once you were a client of ours, we were all part of "being there" for clients, so they could speak to any of our lawyers – free of charge – if any new legal matter arose in their personal or business life. We all do that for our clients, right?

Yes, but we made it a clear and tangible benefit of being a client of ours. As one of our main competitors said to me late one night at a business social event – "You're doing no more than we do. You're just doing it better".

We used these schemes or "clubs" as a springboard to nurture and develop clients – building on the "you are centrally-owned" message that we'd sent out to clients from the outset. For example, where the business was of sufficient size, one of our "ambassadors" would visit corporate clients to get to know them in a non-sales way, and to explore opportunities for us to extend proactive care to them. The message to the clients was strong and long-lasting, and the ambassadors often came back with more cases.

I now work with law firms to set up these schemes or clubs, along with building the "service" differentiator, as part of a wider programme to move them towards being The Perfect Legal Business. Change, at a pace, really is possible.

Going back to the case of the tree (above), in The Perfect Legal Business, neither the Employment lawyer nor the Employment Team own the client. Rather, they are just carrying the baton for the time being. While the baton is carried by the Employment Team on that client's Matter .001, the Employment *Team's* job – and in particular the Employment *Team Leader's* job – is to make sure the Employment lawyer who is dealing with the case delivers a great service in accordance with the firm's Service Pledge. That's how they do their bit for the team.

The individual lawyer's job is to do a great job – to "Push and Tell" – or to put their hand up within their team and to their Team Leader if they aren't able to do either of those things. That will ensure that the Employment Team keep Matter .001, and it will make sure the client considers the firm to be their lawyers should they need anything else.

It will also make them amenable to exploring the proactive care that The Perfect Legal Business extends to all of its clients (see below).

You can hopefully see our differentiators building up.

Firstly, we offered a Service Pledge and a great service – every lawyer, every time. We *all* gave a shit.

Secondly, we offered the central engagement and the "client clubs" or schemes, which came with a range of benefits for personal or business clients. Already, that list is better than "award-winning" and "a Top 100 firm".

But there's more, because thirdly, we offered what I now call our Platforms – proactive care rather than us waiting for the phone to ring. While any team is carrying the baton for a client of the firm – and more than one team can carry a baton for a client at the same time – and whilst the firm is thus delivering an amazing service, so far that's a *reactive* service, responding to a call made by the client. In a law firm, though, there are plenty of opportunities to extend *proactive* care to personal and corporate clients.

Waiting for the phone to ring is putting your clients at risk. As you'll see in the next chapter, a further thing The Perfect Legal Business does, having engaged with a new client in a central way, is not wait for the phone to ring.

CHAPTER 11

PROACTIVE CARE

At law firms I work with, I often ask the Corporate, Commercial, and Real Estate Partners in the room whether they care for their clients. They usually reply emphatically that they do.

I then ask them whether they have ever discussed with their business clients what would happen if the CEO died, or more likely these days, had a heart attack or some other incapacity so that they were alive but without the legal capacity to run their affairs or their business. What would happen to their business, its employees, the director's family, and so on?

Many, many corporate and commercial lawyers have admitted to me that they have *never* asked any of the hundreds of directors they have worked with whether they have all of the available and necessary protections in place.

That's not "caring for clients".

All individuals, adults, and families can be raised onto a platform where the risks they might otherwise face, or the impact of those risks, are reduced. All businesses can similarly be put on a platform where the risks they face, or the impact of those risks, are reduced. I believe there is a great opportunity for law firms to do something life-changing for clients, not by selling to them – but rather by proactively caring for them.

We did this. It works. It is an utterly good thing for a law firm to do.

I have seen that many firms write to conveyancing clients and to matrimonial clients, telling them that they should have a will in place. I have heard many firms talk about offering "free health checks" to businesses.

In spirit, these are both excellent initiatives and embody the approach of The Perfect Legal Business. Most of the time, though, I fear they can come across as less important and valuable to the client than they really could be. They are peripheral to the work being done for a client, not central to it.

As law firms, we sit on life-changing and business-changing awareness, knowledge, and experience. The vast majority of that is only put at the client's disposal when something hits the fan. That is a real shame and a missed opportunity.

At my firm, we wanted to do something about it. For personal clients, we developed something that we called The Portfolio. The Portfolio was a nice branded box file that was given to as many clients as possible. In it was a guide to the clear advantages for them of getting three pieces of paper in place which could change their lives and the lives of their family – a Will, a "Property & Financial" Lasting Power of Attorney, and a "Health" Lasting Power of Attorney.

We didn't sell these things – rather, we implored clients to get them in place, whether it was through our offices or not. It was part of a joined-up, consistent message that we were on the same side as the client. Although there were pricing advantages if a client procured two or more of these documents, they weren't priced low.

Our aim was to have all our clients with their Portfolios in place and all their affairs in order. What was the alternative for clients – dealing with intestacy on death or with the Court of Protection on an incapacity? These bring delays, expense, and uncertainty, heaped on trauma. I recall one occasion when I was working with one law firm's people to get everyone on board and to build up a head of steam on this "proactive care" initiative. A lady in the group became very upset because – at that very time – her family was wrestling with all the ramifications of someone in her family having lost capacity without there being a Lasting Power of Attorney in place. Everything had to be done via the Court of Protection, where response times are measured in months, not hours or days. It reinforced my belief in all that I was doing. Getting clients to "Portfolio" state could be truly life-changing for them.

My wife and I both have our Portfolios on our shelf at home – everything is in order lest the worst happens. It'll save our kids and wider family a fortune in trauma, delays, and expense.

For business clients, the opportunities to help your clients climb onto a platform where they are safer are all the greater. It takes the "free health check" idea and makes it actually happen, but as part of a wider "care" message where your interests are aligned with those of your client rather than being diametrically opposed to them.

"Let us work with you to get you onto a platform where you'll pay lawyers a lot less and where your management time can be spent on positive rather than negative things". Business clients will thank you for helping them get their account-opening procedures, terms and conditions, credit control system, shareholders agreement, and employment contracts all dove-tailed and up-to-date. At a price, of course.

We could thus add this proactive care to our list of differentiators, and I now help firms to design and launch what I actually call their "Platforms". These are tailored to their clients and their expertise and resources. These are so many things at the same time – things to be proud of, differentiators in your marketplace, and generators of good fees.

Where the opportunity here breaks down, of course, is where some lawyers take the view that "My clients are my clients, and you're not selling anything to my clients". That view has no place in The Perfect Legal Business.

How can a lifetime's care, in the broadest sense, be offered and extended to a business client and its owners that have no engagement with a firm other than, say, with one of its property lawyers in respect of its property matters?

As we move to look at the next facet of the Perfect Legal Business, the clue is in the name. *Business*. The firm is extending an amazing service, so it is entitled to make maximum money – in both profit and cash terms – on every case.

CHAPTER 12

MAKING MAXIMUM MONEY FOR DELIVERING AN AMAZING SERVICE

The "profit and cash journey" for law firms is comprised of a series of separate challenges. You have to get all of them right. The chain breaks down at any of its links.

Step 1 – Price the work at the right level

We had every reason to have "Pride in Pricing" – more reason than any firm I know – but we didn't translate the power of our brand and our differentiators into price differentials between us and other firms (in terms of our fixed pricing or our hourly rates). It never occurred to me that we might be able to adopt and instil a confidence across the firm that what we were offering was special and that clients should, therefore, pay a "Bentley" price for it.

Step 2 – Defining retainers and charging an extra price for extra work

When we did do this, it was more to reduce the risk of Professional Indemnity claims against us, rather than to make sure that we never had to do any work for free. I have seen firms use this tool to great effect, where vertical and horizontal definitions are put in place in the retainer to ensure the firm always gets paid for all work it does. By vertical lines, I mean that if the extent of the job widens, extra charges will kick in. By horizontal lines, I mean that regardless of whether the job changes, extra charges will kick in if it goes beyond a certain date, or if time costs exceed the fixed price by a certain percentage.

Step 3 – Do the work

There's no money to be made from storage. If a file isn't being worked on, it's costing you money, not earning you money. It's also costing you your good name.

But there's "working on a file" and there's "working on a file". Snatching a few minutes on a file because the client has chased you or because a deadline is approaching is a far cry from measured, thoughtful, detailed work on a file. A firm often needs more lawyers (or a better team structure) more than it needs more files.

Step 4 – Record all the time you spend on a file (Utilisation)

Chargeable hours and charging by an hourly rate have not gone away. Far from it. From what I see at the many law firms I work with, these are still the mainstay of legal businesses in this country. Simply put, the more chargeable hours a law firm's lawyers properly record, the better the opportunity to generate maximum profit and cash "down the line".

I often see frustration (not just on the part of Management but also on the part of lawyers themselves) when lawyers record no more than 3 or 4 chargeable hours in a day that saw them start work at 8am, work through their lunch, toil hard all day, and go home well into the evening.

One reason for this is that lawyers may simply have too many files. It's hard to catch all the time you spend on a range of files when you are dashing from file to file to file.

It might also be because, in fact, the priority in a firm is not to record as many chargeable hours as possible. Every lawyer may have a "chargeable hours" target – commonly 5 a day, or 1,200 a year – but all the reporting and monitoring and applauding (and barking) that goes on might be around something completely different… billing.

As I did at my firm, many firms focus on the *output* target of "bills raised" instead of focusing firstly on the *input* target of "the number of chargeable hours put into the system". The result is that billing can be much less than it might otherwise be, and hitting billing targets – rather than a desire to hit maximum production – is what drives lawyers. You can hit billing targets without getting anywhere near maximum production (or Utilisation).

In the most general of terms, you might have a three-year qualified solicitor who is paid, say, £40,000 a year. Their hourly rate might be £180 an hour. If they were to focus on recording time in a drive to hit their "chargeable hours" target, then they could easily bill over £200,000 a year. But often what drives them and the team and the firm is a different target – their billing target, and there is a broad view in the legal profession that salaries (S) and billings (B) are the two sides of an equation where B = 3 x S.

This imposes an artificial cap on the billings that lawyers can contemplate and that firms require of their lawyers. In this example, the lawyer might feel it reasonable that they are asked to bill around £120,000, but less reasonable if they are asked to bill over £200,000, in light of the salary they are on.

If, instead of focusing on the *output* of billings, a firm focuses on (and reports on and rewards) the *input* of chargeable hours, the result could (and I say *could*, as there's more to it than this) in due course be much higher billings from the same lawyers with the same cases.

Setting targets on the input rather than the output side would require that the lawyers were more efficient in catching all the time they spend on files – I rarely see lawyers who are anything but very busy with client work – but the upside is much improved financial performance by them individually, by their team, and by their firm as a whole. They would be entitled to expect that as the tide came in, all the boats would rise, and they would benefit.

At my firm, yes, we had a "chargeable hours" target and, yes, the chargeable hours (or Utilisation) data appeared somewhere on a crowded spreadsheet every month. But, frankly, I was only interested in whether each team had hit their monthly billing (output) target. Of course, the team output target was based on the sum of all the output targets allocated to the team's lawyers, based roughly on the B = 3 x S formula.

By focusing on the "time recording" input instead of the "billing" output, you can easily move towards a situation where B = 4 x S or even B = 5 x S, at no extra cost, so that the extra revenue drops straight to the bottom line. The result is a strong business that offers security, rewards, and opportunities to its people.

Step 5 – Billing all time on the billing guide (Realisation)

It's no use recording lots of hours on a file (so that your Utilisation figures are good) that you then write off when it comes to doing a bill. The aim at The Perfect Legal Business is also to bill all the time that is recorded on a billing guide. That is, to have a 100% *Realisation* rate.

There might be a number of reasons why, say, there's £1,000 on the billing guide, but a bill is raised for only £750. These could include an element of double-charging if the file has been transferred between lawyers with consequent reading-in, or mistakes were made that obviously can't be charged for. However, they can also include sympathy for the client or lack of "Pride in Pricing" on the part of the lawyer. I once even had a Partner whose bills were always nice round numbers – they habitually rounded bills down because they "didn't like funny numbers". That must have cost us a fortune.

I recall being guilty of this discounting myself, when I did the monthly billing for a household-name client for whom we were carrying out a lot of work across a lot of teams at any one time. I recall looking for opportunities to offer discounts and reductions, to "throw a bit in" in return for all the other work we were charging for. I had no reason whatsoever to do that – we were blowing the client away with an amazing cross-firm service that they'd never seen before. I have seen many firms – where I look at the reasons behind low Realisation rates – who do the same.

In the same way that low Utilisation "input" rates are overlooked if the "output" billing levels are in line with billing targets (which, in turn, are based only on the $B = 3 \times S$ equation), so too are low Realisation rates. I was guilty of this. Nothing mattered, provided the (low) output targets were hit.

"Ah yes", I hear some lawyers say, "none of this applies to me as all of my work is fixed-fee work".

They couldn't be more wrong.

If lawyers price a fixed-fee job at, say, £1,000, and it always takes £1,500 of time (so that Utilisation rates are high as the lawyers work hard to deal with the cases but the Realisation rates are low because the price being quoted does not take into account all the time the job will require) then the challenge in that fixed fee work is getting the fixed price up – first to £1,100, then to £1,250, and then to £1,500, or more directly. The realisation rate goes up at each stage.

The way to get the price up is to explain to the client *why* the price is higher – by pointing to your differentiators (the greatest of which will be your expertise, your familiarity with their work, and your great service level). Do the clients really want to go back out into the marketplace and have to educate a new firm about their case or their business, and run the risk of engaging a firm that neither pushes nor tells?

What should Utilisation rates and Realisation rates be? The answer is always simply "Higher!" That's the genuine answer – higher. If Team Leaders work with their individual lawyers, within a framework where these inputs are "front of house" and are monitored and rewarded as highly as the billing output was previously, they can slowly but surely get their Utilisation rates up and their Realisation rates up, and the result will be an increase in the output of billing.

Step 6 – Getting paid quickly

There's no point in having the confidence to quote high prices, and of having a culture where the inputs of Utilisation and Realisation are more important than the output of billing, only for that apparatus to result in more and more larger bills finding a home (and travelling to the right) in the "Aged Debtors" list. The more bills and the bigger the bills on this list, the more harm it will do to the business. Growth in billing levels, as I hope is clear from earlier chapters, can cause real pain if the bills aren't paid quickly.

In summary, when it comes to profit and cash, The Perfect Legal Business delivers an amazing service, but it demands a good price in return, in cash terms, from the clients.

The Perfect Legal Business ensures maximum profit by having 'Pride in Pricing' at the outset and by focusing on the lawyers' inputs rather than their outputs as the cases progress. It then avoids undermining the whole show by also having a Cash Commitment.

Now that I am a disciple who worships at the altar of fee-earner inputs rather than outputs, I help firms to buy into this new approach and to get all their lawyers to strive to become more effective and efficient at turning their hard work and great service into profit and cash – and then to go home on time.

I have seen examples with firms I have worked with where, as quickly as Month #1 of the "new way", lawyer performance can go up universally, so that team performances can go up universally, with the effect that the firm's profit goes up. In one case that jumps to mind, we saw the firm's profitability go up every month for the next 6 months, including a December without a single new lawyer, any new marketing initiatives, or an influx of new cases. Firms have sought my guidance on how they might "grow" by 10%. I can look at their data and show how they could grow profit and cash by over 50%. I am used to the firms I work with having record years – not always in "turnover" terms but in "profit" and "cash" terms. It's easy.

The Perfect Legal Business is a high-profit margin, cash business, not a turnover-based credit business. It has the confidence to only take on work that is priced profitably, and to tell clients at the outset that they have to pay their bills on time or they can't enjoy the great service the law firm offers. They have the confidence to sack and, if necessary, sue clients.

I mentioned in the Introduction to this book that the aspects I explore in this chapter were "the golden key" and that I had developed a greater clarity here. Let me tell you what my latest thinking is.

Imagine that in your firm, and in your team and your area of work, a good new case came in. Have you carefully analysed and set out in black and white (a) *what* you need to do, and *how* you need to do it, to ensure you get the maximum fees on that case, and (b) what you need to do and how you need to do it to get the biggest and best result for the client?

Firms have rarely carried out that exercise. But even if they have, although it might at – first glance – appear helpful and make perfect sense, I now see that it's the wrong exercise.

It's the wrong exercise because it is two-dimensional when it needs to be three-dimensional. The missing dimension is *time*. This additional dimension changes everything.

You can map out various methods and disciplines and approaches that a lawyer can follow to get the best result for the firm (in terms of fees) and for the client (in terms of result).

But "the boss" here, namely the business, isn't interested in getting those fees in at some time in the future. All businesses work to financial years, and it is very much in a law firm's interests to ensure that the current – and every – financial year is good. Try telling your bank or your insurers or your people that "It hasn't been a good year, so no pay rises but – not to worry – we've got lots of files where we're going to make lots of money, someday".

Therefore, it's not just about "making maximum money on every case that comes in". Rather, it's about "making maximum money on every case that comes in, but *soon*".

As I say, that changes everything. A Partner with a huge caseload on their desk might well make maximum money on every file – but when will they do that? You

117

can look at the elements I list above and identify those elements – such as team structures, delegation, and "filling vessels" – that not only help the firm to make maximum money, but also enable it to do so soon.

The firm has to play its part here. If it incentivises lawyers to hit personal billing targets, and it doesn't incentivise team behaviours or the collaboration that benefits both the business and its clients, then we all know what'll happen. Correct – no lawyer will let go of any files and the inevitable result will be the "snatching of time" routine that reduces fees, and a delay in the receipt of good money.

Let's look at how we can make maximum money, soon, on every case (and how we achieve this depends on what type of case it is):

A. Time-recording cases – the priorities (and these bear some repetition from earlier in this book) are:

- Set a high hourly rate, based on the firm's differentiators, and the lead lawyer's differentiators. Set out for the caller *why* and *how* they'll get "Bentley Law", before telling them what Bentley Law costs. Show how the lead lawyer's high rate will only apply to senior work – junior work will be done at lower rates. Set out and update the cost estimates accurately.

- Do the work – there's no point in having the file at an agreed-upon high price if it sits there or if time is snatched. Team structures, delegation, and filling vessels increase the billing that can be done and keep the file moving. Everyone wins. Filling vessels is absolutely key. Don't penalise lawyers for giving files and tasks and time on a file to another lawyer. Set team, not individual, targets.

- Record every minute – even the 2025 data from the Law Society shows that lawyers *record* just over three hours a day, on average. They're easily *doing* double that. It's madness and a real shame. The firm should incentivise time recording instead of allocating billing targets that can be hit by a lawyer working mornings only.

- Bill all the time that is recorded. Why give discounts?

- Bill it all regularly – the name of the game is getting good fees in soon. Use WIP and Aged WIP reports – they're the most under-used tool ever!

- Get paid quickly – the money isn't "in" just because it is all billed and all billed regularly. The firm should incentivise good behaviours here rather than congratulate people who have hit (low) billing targets.

B. Fixed fee cases – the priorities (and, again, these bear some repetition from earlier in this book) are:

- Set a high CORE price – rely on the firm and on individual differentiators, and on "time" data gathered from previous, similar jobs

- Define very clearly what that fee covers and doesn't cover

- Do the work – as above

- Any extra work – identify it immediately and agree an extra fee with the client straight away

- Delays – remember, the name of the game is getting the maximum fee and soon, so there is no reason why you should be out of pocket whilst the case is on hold or paused. Agree interim bills on everything.

- Record all time spent – it will inform your pricing and support your pricing discussions with clients going forward

- Get paid quickly – as above.

The firm or the team need to constantly ask themselves the question, "Are we making maximum money, soon?"

If not, any marketing that you do will just bring in cases where you are reducing the fees that the cases generate, and/or you delay the receipt of those fees. Get this bit right, and then turn on the marketing taps.

Of course, when you turn on the marketing taps, you can quickly squeeze things again so that you can no longer make maximum money, soon, on every case.

That is why growth ought not to be in fits and starts but should be an ongoing process where you are constantly creating the capacity and reinforcing your resources (by recruitment, by developing team structures, and by harnessing tech and AI) so that you never stop making maximum money, soon, on every case (not forgetting that the corollary of you doing this will be that you are delivering a great service, every time, to clients).

In the drive to increase the profitability and cash reserves of the whole of The Perfect Legal Business year after year, though, the firm's Leadership and Senior Management that I mentioned earlier, who lead the revolution, recognise that a law firm is not usually one business, but many.

Each area of law, and thus each team, has its own pressures and opportunities. The way to upgrade the profit and cash performance of the whole firm is to focus on each team individually.

However, Management simply cannot push all the required "head" and "heart" aspects that need to be pushed continually across all teams and all lawyers. Frankly, they are unlikely to fully understand the intricacies of each team's commercial environment and marketplace in the way that a team's members might.

A law firm that has the Managing Partner doing everything, where the Managing Partner or CEO has to liaise with all people at all levels across all teams and offices – to make sure all these aspects move forwards all the time – will have limited prospects of sustained success, particularly if the firm grows. The firm's Management will spread thinner and thinner.

What is needed is effective *Middle* Management —
otherwise known as Team Leaders or Heads of
Department. They are one of the real keys to the
success of The Perfect Legal Business, particularly as it
gets bigger.

CHAPTER 13

TEAM LEADERS

I know the head of an extremely large, non-law business. He prides himself on doing nothing. Seriously. It's obviously something of an exaggeration, but he says that he's proud of the fact that he only gets seven emails a day.

The reason he only gets seven emails a day is because his business is made up of seven "lines", each of which has a Head. He has worked hard to ensure that each of the seven Heads accepts responsibility for, and is effective at, running that line as a business, delivering a Gross Profit to the centre. Each Head ensures – in all hard and soft respects – that everyone engaged in that line embodies and embraces the culture, rules, methods, and behaviours of the whole business.

If a Head doesn't do these things personally or is not able to deliver to the business a line or team that does them all, they don't stay as the Head. Simple. How can the business run and grow if a Head doesn't push what Management wants them to push or – worse – does things a different way?

It is this focus and drive, and this assumption of responsibility, that The Perfect Legal Business requires of its Team Leaders. Compare and contrast this with what one might currently find at law firms.

Often, the expectations of a Team Leader in a law firm are not profit-, cash-, or growth-related. Often, it's not actually clear what the role and responsibility of a Team Leader is! I have seen Team Leaders who have been in situ for years – decades, even – where their part of the business has demonstrated little or no growth. Worse still, I have even seen Team Leaders under no threat of losing their position even when that part of the business is in decline, or has a staff turnover problem, or it has real behavioural and compliance and risk issues, or it has significant and perennial debtor issues. Or where it has declared UDI.

They might still be in office because they're an Equity Partner. Or because no one else who is an *Equity Partner* is available to replace them.

Sometimes, Management knows full well that a Team Leader ought not to be the Team Leader but is hamstrung for reasons of familiarity and history from doing anything about it. But the business needs an effective Team Leader at the front of every part of the business. These situations are nettles that have to be grasped.

As I work with firms to move them towards becoming an improved, let alone Perfect Legal Business, these are key moments. If the right type of person is not at the Head of a Team, the firm cannot move forward as an entity.

What I have found is that in many cases, the Team Leaders in question, when it is discussed constructively with them, don't actually want to be Team Leader –

and certainly not with all the "crap" that goes with the position these days. Once they can see what the business needs and that it's a scientific need rather than anything that is personal in any way, the discussion often turns to who else might be better in the role. And it can become clear and accepted that if someone has the right skills and mettle, it matters not that they aren't an Equity Partner. The business needs everyone in the business to do what they can best do for the business. For the person who has been a reluctant Team Leader for years, that might well be a return to full-time fee-earning and to developing the legal skills of the rest of the team – an invaluable contribution.

Whatever the background to a Team Leader situation, though, and whatever course any discussions have to take, it is a landmark moment on the journey for a firm when the Team Leader group – made up of the right Team Leaders – is settled. Now, anything is possible. From crystallising, we can move on to catalysing.

In The Perfect Legal Business, the Team Leader has a clear focus and a clear set of priorities. A standard business-focused agenda guides their work and ongoing engagement with the people in their team. The Agenda at *Team* level looks like this:

Monthly Team Meetings Agenda	
Workloads	Do we have the right number and seniority of lawyers? Anyone got too much or not enough work? Senior lawyers doing junior tasks? Need more juniors/seniors?
All files being worked on as necessary – storage being avoided?	Are we snatching time on some files?
Support Staff	Are our lawyers dealing with non-chargeable admin? More profitable to get someone in to free lawyers up? Any bottlenecks, e.g., typing?
Fee-earner inputs – Utilisation & Realisation	Are we recording good hours and billing them all?
Our team's gross margin	Heading in a good direction?
Existing debtors	Current state of printouts / target for next month's meeting
New debtor issues arising?	Are we making the same mistakes again?
client engagement re: pricing / retainer / payment	Are we doing this? Feedback / share experiences

Monthly Team Meetings Agenda	
Service levels	Are we delivering on the firm's Service Pledge?
Have we referred any clients to other teams?	How was their response and service?
Have other teams referred clients to us?	How was our response and service?

Team Leaders engage with their team in these ways to ensure that the team delivers on all the hard and soft aspects of The Perfect Legal Business (as set out in this book). The Team Leaders also engage monthly *as a group* with the Senior Management Team to report on their team's progress and performance against the requirements that the centre of the business has of it. The Agenda for those Monthly Management Meetings looks like this:

Monthly Team Meetings Agenda	
Team structures Fee-earners / Vessels	Do you each have the right number and seniority of vessels in your teams? Are your vessels overflowing, okay, or empty? Senior lawyers doing junior tasks? Need more juniors/seniors? Need fewer?

Monthly Team Meetings Agenda	
Workloads / File-openings	Is each team thriving and lively, or stagnating? All work being turned around, or is any in "storage"?
Support staff	Are lawyers dealing with non-chargeable admin? Would it be more profitable to get someone in to free lawyers up? Any bottlenecks?
Team Gross Profit Margin (%)	Current levels satisfactory / going up, in each team? If not satisfactory or it's going down, what action is being taken in those teams to get revenue up and/or to get salaries and direct costs down?
Compliance and Risk Management report	Training needs Breaches Complaints and claims
Client engagement skills and training	Are we engaging in an exacting way regarding price / retainer / payment?
Debtors	Current state of each team's debts? Are new

Monthly Team Meetings Agenda	
	debtor problems arising, or is it just legacy debt?
Our Service Pledge	Are we delivering on this in each team?
Membership of our Client Club	Numbers / communications / promotions to members
Platforms	Being promoted / taken up?
People – outstanding performance / poor performance or behavioural issues	Issues that need to be addressed? Star performers / promotion? Appraisal dates

If there are shortcomings in any area, the Team Leader, the Senior Management Team, and the Team Leader Group work together to address and remedy these. Nothing coasts. There is no room here for a plateau, let alone regression.

A main Team Leader function is *active* production management. Let's return to the example of the companies that make cars I used earlier in the book. In their factories, the parts arrive at one end of the building, and there is a carefully-crafted process – and timetable – designed to convert the components into finished cars at the other end as fast as possible. There are people whose role is to time each part of the process, and to innovate and organise and marshal resources to get those times down and to make sure that quality stays "up". That way, instead of "money out", the business benefits from "money in", sooner rather than later.

Now, compare that to what often happens in a law firm. Lots of cases come in at one end of a team, and then, all too often, production is not managed at all. The case is left on a lawyer's desk to be given time and attention when they can find the time or when something urgent arises on a file (or when a client rings to complain). Production management is left to each lawyer.

But they're often simply too busy to do anything other than work at 100 mph and fight fires. Client service can never be consistent enough to constitute a "brand", the firm can never benefit from the client loyalty and "Pride in Pricing" that comes from that, and the chances of wringing a lifetime's value out of a client (and recruiting them into your sales team) are reduced.

A Team Leader can change all of this and take production management out of the hands of the individual lawyers. It shouldn't actually be in their hands.

A Team Leader can engineer the right team structures (by having what I call in this book good "lieutenants" that the senior lawyers trust) and by deft use of much-underused reports like the Inactivity Report or the Aged WIP report. These are the perfect production management tools.

Managed in this way and staffed in this way, the various lawyers at different levels can do great work on the team's files (instead of snatching "one unit" here and there), and the Team Leader can engage with them in what are effectively "production discussions" about the WIP on their Aged WIP reports, to get all WIP billed as soon as possible. This also makes sure cases don't go into storage. Files carrying big blocks of WIP that can't be billed yet, because more work is first needed on the file, can be given the required attention.

In light of the very varied nature of a Team Leader's role and responsibilities, taking into account all the hard and soft inputs and efforts that are required of a Team Leader in The Perfect Legal Business (see the rest of the book for details!) you may find it surprising to hear that the success or otherwise of a Team and its Team Leader can be measured by a single number.

The Team Leader, and the whole team, have a simple speedometer on which they can see how they are doing. It is the $E = MC^2$ of the legal world. Most firms have it but don't use it.

It is to that number that we turn next.

CHAPTER 14

THE ULTIMATE TEAM SPEEDOMETER – GROSS MARGIN

I had the real pleasure a while back of spending some time with a Head of Division from a highly successful global law firm. This person was a Team Leader but on a massive scale. I was with them because I wanted to see how things on that scale really worked. As a Team Leader and part of the firm's "middle management", he had to report to HQ (which was in another country) every month, by email, on the performance of his part of the massive overall business.

The report each month was in a standard form. It consisted of a single number.

If I asked you, "Which business makes the most profit – BP or your local corner shop?", you'd think that it was a ridiculous question, and indeed it is. No useful comparison can be made between the profits made by BP in £ Sterling and those made by the corner shop.

However, if I put the question another way, it becomes much more meaningful: "Between BP and your local corner shop, which is the most profitable?"

There is a universally recognised number that is used the world over to measure the profit-making efficiency of a business or part of a business. It is called Gross Margin. It is a single number expressed as a percentage. It allows you to compare the profit-making efficiency of a global business to that of a small local business. Businesses the world over are obsessed with it. It drives all that they do.

But do you know *your* Gross Margin? Possibly not. It does not feature heavily, if at all, at most law firms.

For us as a profession, *billing* is everything. Turnover! That completely obscures any understanding of a team or a firm's profit. It's also not a good instrument to drive change and business improvement.

The teams' Gross Margins and the firm's overall Gross Margin do often appear on the printouts that the Finance team prepare and publish every month, but they're hidden amongst thousands of other numbers about billing rather than being the compass and the engine room of the business.

So, what is Gross Margin, what is needed to get it to improve, how do we get our people to do those things, and what is the Team Leader's contribution here?

If you want to work out how much *profit* (which is different to *cash*, of course) a *team* makes in £ Sterling, you can simply deduct their salaries from their billings. That gives you their Gross Profit – in £ Sterling. It doesn't take account of central costs and overheads that the business incurs, like rent, rates, gas, electricity, and so on. The aim is to see how good a team is at making profit, out of which profit those central overheads are then paid. I don't include those overheads when I'm trying to see how good a team is at making profit.

But here, we aren't interested in Gross Profit, measured in £ Sterling – we aren't looking here at actual profit but at the team's *profit-making efficiency*. Hence, we need to move on to a second calculation, which starts with the Gross Profit that you have just calculated.

If you divide the team's Gross Profit (£) by the team's billings (also £), and multiply the answer by 100, you arrive at the team's *Gross Margin*, which is expressed not in £ but as a percentage.

The Gross Margin shows you what percentage of a team's billings exceed the salaries that have been paid up to that point in the financial year to generate those billings. It is a measure of its profit-making efficiency.

And what should a team's Gross Margin percentage be? Higher! That really is the answer. Whatever the Gross Margin is at the moment, the Team Leader's role is to influence – in the right direction – either or both of the only two factors that can make the Gross Margin go up (i.e., to get billings up, or to get salaries down).

"But what if one team's Gross Margin is a lot higher than another team's?" I'm often asked. That's always going to be the case. It's not a comparison you should make – it's irrelevant. We need to ascertain a team's Gross Margin not so we can compare one team to another. Rather, we use the figure so that we can compare a team this month to the same team last month. The strongest and best-performing team in The Perfect Legal Business model is not the team with the highest Gross Margin. It is the team whose Gross Margin improves month after month after month.

Looking at the calculations we've just been through above, you can see the only two factors that can impact

Gross Margin are (1) the billings of the team, and (2) the salaries of the team. The Team Leader has to drive billings up, or they have to drive salaries down. The latter can have a small and slow effect on the team's Gross Margin. The former can have a huge and rapid effect on it.

In a nutshell, the Team Leader's main role, therefore, in The Perfect Legal Business, is to drive the team's billings up. And that is done by all the ways we examine in this book – having only good people in the team, Pride in Pricing, good Utilisation by the lawyers (chargeable hours), good Realisation levels by the lawyers (no write-offs), adhering to the Service Pledge, and having the right team structures in place so that file storage is avoided.

And, of course, profit is something that exists only on paper until bills are paid – the Team Leader's job is forever to be the cash policeman, too.

I suspect that if the Team Leader kept the "crown jewel" that is the team's Gross Margin to himself or herself, it'd be a bit like pushing a rock up a hill in the dark. Far from keeping it secret, therefore, I advocate that ownership of a team's Gross Margin is passed to the whole team. They then see it as a measure of their own collective business efficiency, and they will hopefully adopt the team-like behaviours and priorities necessary to get the Gross Margin up – particularly if those behaviours are enshrined in the firm's reward and promotions apparatus.

Where a firm goes on a business-improvement journey, a team's Gross Margin can improve in Month #1. That of all teams can. The Perfect Legal Business constantly uses this measure of business efficiency to make sure that it doesn't slip in any quarter, or – if it does – that the Team Leader quickly takes remedial action.

The Perfect Legal Business, therefore, works hard – through its Team Leaders and through the performance of its people – to drive profitability on every case and in every team. It also ensures that all profitability is turned into cash.

But if we stopped there, all we'd have is a business that dealt well and profitably with any case that came in.

There's a final piece to The Perfect Legal Business jigsaw. For, just as one case completes, another is needed. The final difference between the Perfect Legal Business and an imperfect one, is where the Perfect Legal Business looks as a priority to find those new cases.

CHAPTER 15

GETTING TO .007 AND BEYOND

Wearing many hats, I have been the client of many law firms over the decades, as have my family, my businesses, my friends, and my many business Partners.

Although many lawyers have great relationships with their clients, it is not unusual for the relationship to be a transactional one rather than a "wider relationship" one. A client engages with a lawyer to get their affairs in order, to deal with a divorce, to buy a house, to manage their property portfolio, to acquire a business, or to deal with a Tribunal case. If there is one, the relationship is often between the client and a particular lawyer in a firm, rather than between the client and the firm as a whole.

The result of this can be that different Partners in a team can have their own client banks, and different teams in a firm can have their own client banks. Each bank is owned by a team, or by individual lawyers in the teams.

Following on from this, it is not unusual that a client (particularly a corporate client) might use more than one law firm for their various legal needs.

Firms are often surprised when I ask them to map out the work that they get *and don't get* from their Top 100 clients. They can do this with what I call a Client Matrix (also called a Gap Analysis), which might – in its simplest form – look like this:

Client	Dispute Res Fees	Real Estate fees	Employment fees	Corp fees
A	25,000			
B		14,000		
C				120,000
D	125			
E			19,000	

This is not an unusual sight – I see it at every firm I work with. It represents one of the easiest opportunities to find profit-rich and cash-rich growth. It beats the many roads that firms travel down in order to secure growth, which we looked at earlier in this book.

What does the above table tell you? It tells me:

- The firm has had a big litigation case for Client A. What an opportunity to get under the skin of that business and to show how your firm will fight for its clients.

- One of the Real Estate Partners who looks after Client B is wittingly or unwittingly keeping them to himself or herself.

- The Corporate team had a big deal on for Client C. If it was a sale, the client has probably gone (but were the owners looked after and did they have all their affairs in order?). If it was a purchase, just imagine how much legal work the enlarged business will have.

- The firm has had one small debt recovery matter from Client D – what a great opportunity to start a relationship with the Finance Director.

- The Employment Partner who looks after Client E is wittingly or unwittingly keeping them to himself or herself.

All the while, the Employment, Real Estate, Dispute Resolution, and Corporate Teams are meeting with the Marketing team to look at ways for them to try to win new clients. That is – new clients whose Matter .001's will come into *their* team.

The Perfect Legal Business does not focus on winning new .001's like this. It's hard work, it's expensive, it's uncertain, and it attracts new clients whose first question will often be, "What's your best price?"

The Perfect Legal Business instead focuses on making sure that it gets all the legal work that all of its clients have. And it will have a good chance of getting all their work, too, because it has nothing but very good lawyers who deliver a very good service – every lawyer, every time. A Partner doing, say, Employment work for a company client is not going to come up against much resistance when he invites the client to engage with his Property and Corporate colleagues, too.

But this colleague-to-colleague internal market won't develop if the culture in a firm is against it. For example, if a colleague in one team simply doesn't trust the work or service levels of a colleague in another team (or of a whole team – it happens), you cannot expect them to involve that colleague (or team) in the clients they have long looked after so well. That's why the Perfect Legal Business has nothing but good lawyers across the firm – so that every lawyer trusts every lawyer.

It also won't work if the firm has a "staff turnover" issue. If you have a lawyer with a nice basket of lucrative clients who cannot be certain that he or she is going to be staying at the firm, the last thing they're going to do is bring their basket of clients into the centre of the firm. And you won't get it if individual lawyers think they own their clients.

Colleague-to-colleague introductions are fine and can be effective, but I have seen that there are never as many of these as you would like there to be. Everyone's too busy. Instead, there has to be *central* access to all clients – access that is unfettered by over-protective, territorial Partners.

If the broad "all round care, for the long term" message is strong, and the clients are brought into the centre of the firm rather than being put in a silo, and they're brought into a client club that flies a broad firm flag rather than a narrow "team" flag, and the service that every lawyer delivers is a great service, then the ground is very fertile for harvesting a wider crop from every client.

This will happen naturally if all the above parts of the jigsaw are in place – but there's no harm in moving things on a little. The Platforms discussed above will help here – they can really accelerate your way towards Matter .007 for every client.

So can the Client Matrix and Gap Analysis – targeted marketing to particular clients in relation to particular work-types. Instead of setting up a conference and then wondering who to invite to it, it can be as easy as identifying 100 existing clients for whom you don't do Employment work, and setting up a conference for them.

In all of this, the Marketing team would work with those lawyers who were carrying or who had carried the baton for a client (and who had delivered the knockout service to them).

So, saying that the Perfect Legal Business focuses on its existing clients rather than on new clients is not saying that Marketing has no role, and it is not to say that Marketing and the lawyers don't work together. Quite the opposite – Marketing's role and workload is enhanced, as is the teamwork between them and the lawyers in the firm.

New cases from new clients (.001's) come at a price and sometimes without profit. Compare and contrast .007's, which come from "repeat" clients that you already know as a firm, and who have already proved their value to you as paying, value-buying clients.

Instead of celebrating new client acquisitions (the profitability of whose work may be dubious when you take into account the hard bargain they've driven and all the "added value" that they wanted "throwing in"),

The Perfect Legal Business has as one of the KPIs that everyone in the firm owns and tracks "Percentage of clients at .007".

What's the point in adding another .001 to a pile of work that is already too high for you to service properly and profitably?

Based on my experience, I am a firm believer in the proposition that .007 is where it's at. It is indeed a License to Bill.

CHAPTER 16
PULLING ALL OF THIS TOGETHER

There you have it. My take on what makes The Perfect Legal Business. Or at least *a* Perfect Legal Business. It might be very different to what you expected or to what you might feel "the perfect legal business" should look like.

It's certainly very different to the firm I set about building back in 2007. The "heart" bits are all exactly the same, but what features more prominently now are the various "head" parts – the harder "business" aspects.

I stand proudly by the things we did that changed the lives of our clients and our people, but those were great traits of "the perfect firm of solicitors".

That is to forget (and it is often said that the *legal profession* forgets) what *business* is all about. Business is all about money – specifically, profit *and* cash.

There is no getting away from the fact, nowadays, that to carry on being the "perfect firm of solicitors", you absolutely have to be "the perfect legal *business*", too.

As I said to the firm that was about to open a Dubai office because all their competitors were doing so, but which had a massive Debtors ledger, "Get the basics right at home, and you'll never look back. Don't roll out an engine that's firing on just two or three cylinders".

The areas I was referring to are all the chapters in this book, but in the simplest terms, what I meant was:

- Do a great job for every client, every case

- Make clients' lives better, not worse

- Choose your clients carefully and set the rules

- Choose your people carefully, and make them fly

- Get everyone rowing the boat in the same direction

- Get rid of anyone who is drilling holes in the boat

- Nothing happens by accident – you need good Management and Middle Management

- Set a good price for your amazing service

- Be your clients' lawyers, not just their lawyer

- Don't be ashamed of making money – it will allow you to change even more lives

- Focus on lawyer inputs, not outputs

- Only one type of "money" counts – cash

- Don't hide the stuff you can do for clients that will save them trauma and money

If you do all of that, clients and talent will be knocking on your door to get in, and none will want to get out.

By strengthening these essentially internal aspects, your external power and magnetism is strengthened, too.

You will be The Perfect Legal Business.

All of which brings us not to THE END, but to THE BEGINNING.

For The Perfect Legal Business, growth comes easily – and it really is growth of the right sort.

Simon McCrum, 2025

Other Books from Simon McCrum

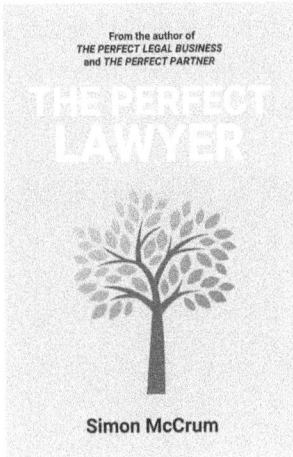

The Perfect Lawyer

From the author of
THE PERFECT LEGAL BUSINESS
and *THE PERFECT PARTNER*

THE PERFECT LAWYER

Simon McCrum

What makes a perfect lawyer? To start answering this question, we need to use a classic lawyer approach - it depends!

In *The Perfect Lawyer*, Simon deep dives into what makes a perfect lawyer in a perfect legal business. It is someone who does a great job from the client's perspective but also does a great job from their law firm's – and they are very different things. When combined effectively, such lawyers not only change their clients' lives, but also the destiny of the legal business they work in, and the lives of themselves and their colleagues.

Whether you are part of a large legal firm or a small one, the themes explored in *The Perfect Lawyer* examine the symbiosis between a law firm's team members and the organisation, as they both evolve into higher-earning and more effective entities.

Note: *The Perfect Lawyer* is the sister book to *The Perfect Legal Business* in that it looks at many of the same themes, but from the viewpoint of the individual lawyer. As such, it contains material that crosses both titles. As you already have a copy of *The Perfect Legal Business*, you won't need *The Perfect Lawyer*.

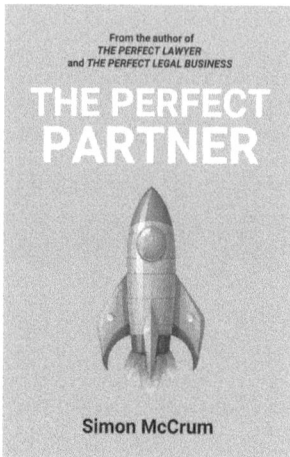

The Perfect Partner

If you've made it to Partner, or you're determined to become one, what are the key qualities and strengths required of a Partner in a modern-day law firm?

In *The Perfect Partner*, Simon examines what makes a Perfect Partner from the viewpoint of numerous key stakeholders, including clients, colleagues, and the business itself. Detailing the characteristics and behaviours that a Partner needs, the book digs deep into a Partner's commercial contribution to the business, their relationships with staff and other Partners, business development, accountability, compliance, and much more. And all under the central umbrella of making a profit and growing a business.

Working through the layers of value (or destruction) that a Partner can bring, Simon arrives at a surprising conclusion. Measurable things count, but other more human things *count more*. If that law firm rocket is going to take off, and prove able to shoot for the stars, each Partner – and all the Partners together – need to focus unequivocally on a 'magic ingredient' to make the firm unstoppable.

Have you got what it takes to be a Perfect Partner? And, just as importantly, have your Partners got the right stuff, too?

www.ingramcontent.com/pod-product-compliance
Lightning Source LLC
Chambersburg PA
CBHW041145230326
41599CB00039BA/7182